Overly Verbal Ape
Studies in the Work of SJ Fowler

Wilfred Franklin & Julia Rose Lewis

NEWTON-LE-WILLOWS

Published in the United Kingdom in 2025
by The Knives Forks And Spoons Press,
51 Pipit Avenue,
Newton-le-Willows,
Merseyside,
WA12 9RG.

ISBN 978-1-916590-16-8

Copyright © Wilfred Franklin & Julia Rose Lewis 2025.

The right of Wilfred Franklin & Julia Rose Lewis to be identified as the author of this work has been asserted by them in accordance with the Copyrights, Designs and Patents Act of 1988. All rights reserved. No part of this publication may be reproduced, stored in a retrieval system, transmitted in any form or by any means, electronic, photocopying, recording or otherwise, without prior permission of the publisher.

Acknowledgements:

'Elaborate Biological Filigrees' was published in HVTN Magazine Substack (https://hvtn.substack.com/p/elaborate-biological-filigrees?utm_source=email).

'Can an orangutan be too shrewd?' was published in Seed: Objects of Wonder Journal, Issue 4.

'Kin Listener' was published on the online edition of Overground Underground (https://overgroundunderground.co.uk/blog/f/kin-listener).

'Hieratic Monkey: SJ Fowler's Performance at the BSB April Launch' was published by the Journal of British and Irish Innovative Poetry 15(1). (https://poetry.openlibhums.org/article/id/9048/)

Contents

Kin Listener — 1

Hieratic Monkey — 7

Elaborate Biological Filigrees — 15

Can an orangutan be too shrewd? — 21

If Fulfilling Then Family — 31

Unfoldingorilla — 43

A Palimpsest Ape — 53

Overly Verbal Ape

Kin Listener

The half-art, half-instinct of language still bears the stamp of its gradual evolution.[1]

Minton is the king whisperer, beginning with some magnificent whispers. We hear and read these sounds as a way of calling Fowler to him as a chimpanzee might call out the discovery of fruit trees. Minton is signaling the promise of something fruitful to come. The opening encapsulates their shared history, beginning with the Feral Choir. Fowler and Minton's performance is different in the sense that they have become each other's ideal listener here.

Fowler is the kind whisperer in the beginning of the duet. It is important to note that he is hosting the event which creates a kind of liminal double of himself. He is both human and chimpanzee. Fowler's whimpering should not only be interpreted as an expression of his emotional state or pure imitation of chimps, it is giving the audience information about his relationship to Minton. The whimpering sounds he emits signal his position in the social hierarchy relative to Minton. He is identifying himself as more junior and lower in prestige. It is not uncommon for male chimps to form close friendships even and especially when they have unequal social status. In this performance, professional status is equated with social group hierarchy to reveal the similarities between literary scene and the forest.

Fowler and Minton are commenting on the nature of community and the community of nature in listening. Their familiarity is made a metaphor for the relationship between chimpanzees and humans. We felt that we were observing an interaction in the way a scientist might observe two highly intelligent individuals and it felt immaterial to us whether they were chimpanzees or humans. This discussion of literary and primate community building is especially well suited to the university setting. It does not matter whether the students are poets or anthropologists. Fowler and Minton performed their duet as part of the Writers Kingston event #49 Sound Poetry

---

1. Charles Darwin, *The Descent of Man, and Selection in Relation to Sex* (London, United Kingdom: John Murray, 1871)

and Sonic Literature February Tuesday 1st 2022: Town House Building at Kingston University, London; an event open to the public and recorded.[2]

The performance reflects the current state of primatology to the experimental poetry audience. Fowler and Minton's work represents the absolute best of interdisciplinarity by insisting on keeping up with other fields and refracting those understandings through the lens of their own. In their book, *The First Idea: How Symbols, Language, and Intelligence Evolved from Our Primate Ancestors to Modern Humans,* Greenspan and Shanker describe the complexity of primate communication. They write:

> We are only just starting to understand the subtlety and importance of that gestures, body movements, facial expressions, and posture play in creating and maintaining individual social relationships and group cohesion amongst chimpanzees and bonobos. It is clear, however, that the social organization of chimpanzees and bonobos is far more complex than was thought a generation ago.[3]

The duet asked the audience to consider the twin questions; what is the evolution of literature and what is the literature of evolution? Experimental also known as avant-garde poetry is especially concerned with the evolution of literature. Interdisciplinary work drawing on poetry and biology might be called experimental, because it transcends the boundaries that traditionally define poetry. What does literature contribute to our understanding of evolutionary theory?

Phil Minton has made himself a kind listener. Not for listening to those in positions of power, rather, for empowering those who might otherwise not have been heard. He conducts a series of workshops for people interested in vocal work and performance. Minton writes that the project originated with non-singers. This phrase can be understood as a parallel construction to non-fiction, following the pattern of negation and genre. Minton is interested in how non-singers can be present with one another without words. His work aligns with Grobstein and Lesnick's thesis in *Education Is Life Itself: Biological Evolution as a Model for Human Learning.* They write: 'what drives the learning process is not a pre-conceived, conscious, discrete goal to be reached in the future but rather an engaged and situated exploration

---

2. SJ Fowler and Phil Minton, 'Phil Minton and SJ Fowler : Sound Poetry at Writers Kingston', Youtube [1st February 2022] < https://www.youtube.com/watch?v=7IYz_n1jK4I> [accessed 10th February 2022]

3. Stanley Greenspan and Stuart Shanker, *The First Idea: How Symbols, Language, and Intelligence Evolved from Our Primate Ancestors to Modern Humans* (Boston, Massachusetts: Da Capo Press, 2006)

in the present'.[4] They are asking how bi-directional exchange can lead to deeper reflection.

The Feral Choir has taken Minton around the world to run a series of vocal workshops and performances that privileges a desire to experiment over experience. The name, Feral Choir, is very much a manifesto in miniature. The juxtaposition of feral and choir suggests that a group of people could come together to exercise their voices outside of tradition and dogma. Minton writes that 'in the workshops [he has] encouraged participants to realize that anyone who can breathe, is capable of producing sounds that give a positive aesthetic contribution to the human condition and many of these contributions are without any cultural influences or references'.[5] As Minton has made huge strides towards empowering people to express themselves in a musical and vocal format that might not have access to traditional training or be in possession of what is traditionally defined as a good voice.

Fowler is the king listener. He is using sound poetry not simply to imitate, but to develop a greater sympathy for chimpanzees within himself and without the audience. Fowler's exploration of chimpanzee vocalizations has been an ongoing project. When reflecting on his participation in the Feral Concord at Cafe Oto in February 2018 he considers the difference between solo and collaborative performance. Fowler writes that he is 'therefore often at a remove, which is a grand thing most of the time, but also cautious, in this case, to not be the chimp whistling when others are singing or singing when others are whistling'.[6] This conflating of human and chimpanzee sounds is intentional. Fowler is illustrating the complex dynamics of an improvisational collaborative performance by representing himself as a chimpanzee and the other performers as humans.

There were moments in this duet when we thought Fowler and Minton were both chimpanzees, one human listening to a chimpanzee, and both humans. It was not only sound, but body language in the juxtaposition of rapid movements of Fowler's mouth with soft to almost imperceptible sounds. Minton is rocking his torso side to side moving himself nearer and farther to Fowler giving a kind of punctuation to the exchange. Frequently, their eyes are closed and in these moments the audience is most aware of itself as something to present to be blocked out. The audience is most like visitors to a zoo at this moment. The very sense of energy existing between them, rather than between them and the audience made me want to lean in closer. The softness of the sounds they made intensified this desire to lean into the

---

4. Paul Grobstein and Alice Lesnick, 'Education Is Life Itself: Biological Evolution as a Model for Human Learning.', *Evolution: Education and Outreach*, 4.4, (2011), 688-700.
5. Phil Minton, *Feral Choir - Phil Minton* (2022) <https://www.philminton.co.uk/feral-choir> [accessed 25th March 2022]
6. SJ Fowler, *A note on: being in a Feral Concord* (2022) <http://www.stevenjfowler.com/blog/2018/10/3/a-note-on-being-in-a-feral-concord> [accessed 23rd March 2022]

performance and close up the space. We suspect that this was a conscious choice on their part to remind the audience of the subtlety possible in sound poetry. There is a listener-whisperer dichotomy here.

Fowler and Minton take turns alternating as listener and whisperer. However, there is a deeper meaning to the term whisperer when one is considering kinships beyond the humans. Fowler is approaching the problem of chimpanzee vocal anatomy from the opposite direction taken in the scientific community. He is asking if human beings can make the same sounds as chimpanzees. Here the very ambiguity mirrors our incomplete knowledge of our evolutionary history with primates and the legacy of Jane Goodall's work at Gombe Station. She discovered that chimpanzees engage in toolmaking as well as tool use. Her research helped redefine humanity by contrast. This shifting identity of chimpanzees and humans is an important feature of Fowler's commentary on the state of primatology. He is reminding everyone outside this field of study why it matters.

The audience members are eavesdropping on this discussion of evolution and literature where Fowler and Minton are each other's ideal listeners. In this sense, the audience would be observing anthropologists, biologists, literary critics, and poets. Fowler and Minton are showing and telling how literature evolves by assuming the roles of chimpanzees and humans. The audience is more or less visiting a zoological garden, where the differences and similarities between chimpanzees and humans are displayed. This is a zoo in the intense and unfamiliar sense, where a collection of wild animals or behaviors are found. The wild is brought into society in a zoo and is the exact opposite of the feral. Recall that a feral is born into domestication and returns to the wilderness while a zoo animal is born into the wild and removed to the domesticated place. The zoo animal has the opposite life experience of the feral animal. The fact that Fowler and Minton's duet can sustain these two opposing interpretations speaks to the richness of their work. Together they are feral, fearless, and exploring the question: what does evolutionary theory contribute to our understanding of literature?

Works Cited

Darwin, Charles, *The Descent of Man, and Selection in Relation to Sex* (London, United Kingdom: John Murray, 1871)

Fowler, SJ, *A note on: being in a Feral Concord* (2018) <http://www.stevenjfowler.com/blog/2018/10/3/a-note-on-being-in-a-feral-concord> [accessed 23rd March 2022]

Fowler, SJ, and Phil Minton, 'Phil Minton and SJ Fowler : Sound Poetry at Writers Kingston', Youtube [1st February 2022] < https://www.youtube.com/watch?v=7IYz_n1jK4I> [accessed 10th February 2022]

Greenspan, Stanley, and Stuart Shanker, *The First Idea: How Symbols, Language, and Intelligence Evolved from Our Primate Ancestors to Modern Humans* (Boston, Massachusetts: Da Capo Press, 2006)

Grobstein, Paul, and Alice Lesnick, 'Education Is Life Itself: Biological Evolution as a Model for Human Learning.', *Evolution: Education and Outreach*, 4.4, (2011), 688-700

Minton, Phil, *Feral Choir - Phil Minton* (2018) <https://www.philminton.co.uk/feral-choir> [accessed 25th March 2022]

Hieratic Monkey

Birth is the vase found in between the outlines of evolution and religion. Hieratic refers to the script of ancient Egyptian priests and it is a homophonic translation of the high erratic behavior evoking the monkey swinging from tree to tree. SJ Fowler is the face for monkeys and priests. When he puts himself before the mirror he seizes a monkey seeing a priest and priest staring back at a monkey. Face to face outlines a vase.

Evolution is the vase found in between the outlines of birth and literature. Descent with modification was employed by Darwin and others to describe his theory before the term evolution was popularized and foregrounds the link with birth. The third is given to literature about birth and evolution. In the following we will consider the faces of birth, evolution, grief, literature, religion, and the ways in which they can be combined to give vases. This is based in the ambiguous figure Rubin's vase-face, which is an important part of gestalt psychology.[1] The two faces, or the vase, is seen depending on what is identified for the love of figure and ground. Vases, mirrors, apes, oh my! Neurobiologist Paul Grobstein writes, 'ambiguity and uncertainty are not ... the ripples of the imperfect glass through which the brain tries to perceive reality'.[2] It is common to move from perceiving the two faces to the vase and back again and so ambiguous figure introduce uncertainty. The latin root for ambiguous is doubtful.

Literature is the vase found in between the outlines of birth and grief. A book launch is giving birth to a work of literature, giving it over to the greater world. SJ Fowler organized a launch event for Broken Sleep Books at St John's Church on Bethnal Green April 7th 2022.[3] He was launching his poetry collection, *The Great Apes*, and Bob Bright, Ailsa Holland, Chris

---

1. Elisa Filevich et al. 'Seeing Double: Exploring the Phenomenology of Self-Reported Absence of Rivalry in Bistable Pictures', *Frontiers in human neuroscience* vol. 11 301, 9th June 2017, doi:10.3389
2. Paul Grobstein, 'Getting It Less Wrong, The Brain's Way: Science, Pragmatism, and Multiplism', *INTERPRETATION AND ITS OBJECTS: Studies in the Philosophy of Michael Krausz*, ed. by Andreea Deciu Ritivoi (New York, New York: Rodopi, 2003), p. 161.
3. SJ Fowler, *The Great Apes*, online video recording, YouTube, 7th April 2022, <https://www.youtube.com/watch?v=RtvyEdlG5ec> [accessed 12th April 2022]

Kerr aided in his performance. There were six other readers from Broken Sleep Books: Rishi Dastidar, Fiona Larkin, Alice Wickenden, George Ttoulli, Peter Zavada, and Stuart McPherson.[4] The cover of *The Great Apes* features a primate skull; it is covered with grief, literally, and the birth as a book launch is metaphorical.[5]

Grief is the vase found in between the outlines of evolution and religion. Language is a mirror to the world as it is delineated by the agent the poet the priest. The poet takes the rug that the priest stands on, sits his stuffed great apes on top, and then pulls the rug and apes onto himself. The poet is concealed by the image he has created. The image stands in for *The Great Apes* book that Fowler is launching. Here is the mirror image as a series of physical objects and not merely a metaphor. Let us see apes and monkeys as agents. Fowler makes the rug into a nest for resting, he has made the church into a forest. The elevated space is analogous to a tree. So the performance ends with the poet occupying the position of the priest in the church, using the rug as a blanket. Is this is the literature of evolution or is it returning the literary event to the realm of humanity alone? The poet leaves the audience sleeping with a stuffed animal primate, a remembrance. It is a refusal, a remixing of hierarchy in that the primate and the priest end standing over the poet as ghosts.

Religion is the vase found in between the outlines of birth and literature. The poet gives birth to himself as an orangutan in order to give birth to his latest poetry collection, *The Great Apes*. Fowler takes off his boots, both pairs of socks, and the microphone. He continues taking off his coat, turning it inside out, and putting it back on his body. The shearling coat becomes extensive with his own hair, putting that mullet to good use; the coat becomes him. He becomes the orangutan. He becomes a nonhuman primate to remind us that our history is always inside us.

Literature is the vase found in between the outlines of evolution and religion. He was always a primate. The word primate has religious and zoological meanings. A primate is a chief bishop of the anglican church or a member of the order of mammals including apes, bushbabies, humans, lemurs, marmosets, monkeys, and tarsiers.[6] Primate might be a contronym. Consider the hysterical opposition to the teaching of evolution in American schools and the Scopes Monkey Trial. Fowler running under the rug the first time is foregrounding the hierarchy of the anglican church and reminding the audience of its position as the congregation.

---

4. SJ Fowler, A Note on Launching Great Apes By Being an Ape, <https://steven-fowler-1pys.squarespace.com/blog/2022/4/13/a-note-on-launching-great-apes-by-being-an-ape> [accessed 10th April 2022]

5. Broken Sleep Books, 'SJ Fowler - The Great Apes', *Broken Sleep Books*, 30 April 2022 <https://www.brokensleepbooks.com/product-page/sj-fowler-the-great-apes> [accessed 1st May 2022]

6. Editors of the Oxford English Dictionary, 'Primate', *Oxford English Dictionary*, <https://www.oed.com/dictionary/primate_n1?tab=meaning_and_use#28339980> [accessed 2nd May 2022]

Religion is the vase found in between the outlines of birth and grief. The primate worships the greatest of the stuffed animal primates and takes it onto the dais to worship again. Here is the primate of primates. The primate and the primate of the primate listen to the poet Chris Kerr read from *The Great Apes*. The primate of the primate wipes the primate's eyes as tears born on his face. The tears leave his eyes behind. The primate and the primate of the primate and / or offspring worship the fire and then they blow out the candle the man lit for his brother. The primate rushes under the rug and pulls it over himself as if to hide his face from his face, humans, and the nonhuman primates. The rug suggests the forest habitat that is between disturbed and destroyed for the primates. Here is a gesture toward embarrassment. It disrupts the seated nonhuman primates as the primate buries himself beneath them as the humans were disturbed by his actions. His shame is manufactured to test the limits of empathy among the audience. The audience is immersed and mirrored. We want to attribute this action to savagery and lack of human decency in experimental poetry, in performance art, in Fowler's representation of non-human primates. And yet, did he not bring the grief and religion into the performance as he brought the audience into sympathy with the man and his deceased brother? He foregrounded this act of grieving in his own book launch.

Grief is the vase found in between the outlines of birth and evolution. The stuffed animal primates that Fowler has brought into the church illustrate his offspring. The stuffed animals stand in for the book he is launching as a baby and he throws his stuffed animals out into the church. Julia Rose Lewis was sitting near where one landed and tempted with a measure of human selfishness to keep it. Why do we label this desire human? Because humans have stolen ape offspring to use for scientific experiments. During the intermission, the primate asked, host to audience, poet to human for everyone to return his stuffed animals. His use of stuffed animals is more than necessity, it is a reference to the legendary researcher Jane Goodall who also utilizes stuffed animals in her talks about biodiversity, extinction, and primates. The Jane Goodall Institute names combating wildlife trafficking and illegal trade as one its projects.[7] The primate asks humans if we will continue to consume nature and its creatures knowing as we do that we will consume ourselves? Or do we invite the monkeys into the church?

Birth is the vase found in between the outlines of grief and literature. There is care here. The primate brings out a simian companion, first facing it and then setting it down facing the audience. The term simian refers to monkeys, humans, apes, oh my! Fowler becomes more excited, vocalizing and performing several monkey rolls. He is importing the martial arts term monkey roll. Humans use monkeys as the vehicle of a metaphor for a

---

7. Jane Goodall Institute, 'PROJECT ISSUE: WILDLIFE TRAFFICKING & ILLEGAL TRADE', *Jane Goodall Institute*, <https://www.janegoodall.org/wildlife-trafficking-trade/> [accessed 15th April 2022]

movement or a response. This illustrates how humans have been influenced by monkeys. Fowler is suggesting that humans look on great apes as great apes look on monkeys, so he must become a monkey on this night. He is holding up a mirror to humanity. The primate is vocalizing intensely as he faces the stuffed animals as though he is trying to get the attention of this group of primates strewn all over the rug. He is beckoning them to follow him to higher ground on the stairs. The primate brings the rug down the stairs and arranges a series of nonhuman primates facing the audience in the pews and the poets in the pews reading from *The Great Apes*. Bob Bright, Ailsa Holland, Chris Kerr are facing and reading to Fowler's personal collection of stuffed animals.

Literature is the vase found in the between the outlines of birth and religion. The poets were stationary as they read from *The Great Apes*. Publication of a collection makes the poems fixed to the page and stationary. Here however is the primate. He exits the building extending the boundaries of the event; it is doors and mirrors all the way down. The primate is lost to the audience through the door in a moment that echoes the grief of primates lost to human activity. Grief is the boundary that defines the space outside the forest for primates. In the *Poetics of Space*, Gaston Bachelard discusses how the inside of a house works on its occupants. This is the very boundary that defines a human in a home. He writes:

> How concrete everything becomes in the world of the spirit when an object, a mere door, can give images of hesitation, temptation, desire, security, welcome and respect. If one were to give an account of all the doors one has closed and opened, of all the doors one would like to re-open, one would have to tell the story of one's entire life.[8]

Birth is the first exit and death is the second door. Doors and reflections are both boundaries essential to human thought. The space between the faces of Bright, Holland, Kerr, and Fowler falls entirely behind the audience for a time. The reading is occurring inside and outside St John's on Bethnal Green. His leaving the church and returning is mirrored in the post script to the performance when he lights the candle that he had blown out.

Religion is the vase found in between the outlines of evolution and literature. The second intense vocalization comes as the primate turns his back to the human audience, so that he is back-to-back with the stuffed animals. Here is facing toward the most sacred part of the church with images of christ and the cross. He is a monkey speaking to the anglican god. The quick and dirty way to tell the difference between an ape and a monkey is the presence of a tail. The primate himself referred to the performance as monkey sounds,

---

8. Gaston Bachelard, *Poetics of Space*, trans. Maria Jolas (Boston, MA: Beacon Press, 1994) p. 224.

rather than ape sounds, to further expand the number of species present. Fowler brings evolutionary theory into the church through literature as though poetry can be a lake that dissolves the conflict between evolution and religion. The resulting event is a transdisciplinary solution. The event is turned into a reservoir. There is room enough for anglicans, apes, human faiths, and monkeys to sustain themselves with this solution, this water. Fowler is suggesting that evolution is as essential as water.

Evolution is the vase found in between the outlines of birth and grief. If it is born, then it deserves the attention of literature and religion. See the evolution of literary kinds. Extending the range of human sympathies through experimental poetry is an important part of Fowler's curatorial and poetic practice. He has expanded the boundaries of human experience in Poem Brut. He writes that the project 'roots it's activities in a mindful thinking through of the potentials and possibilities of neurological and physiological diversity for a literature that expands our understanding of what the medium can do'.[9] He has created a greater field to reflect the nature of lived experience, perception, and poetry. It is a meeting place for dyslexics and migraineurs, among others. The primate performance itself comes full circle to ask poets who among them is worthy to read as opposed to sit in the audience. The intense miniature hierarchies within the poetry world are present at book launches. Of course, the poet launching their book is being celebrated as the first poet and the poets in the audience are not even recognized. This rigid hierarchal thinking is utterly disrupted by the primate. He is and is not the poet, he is and is not alone, he is and is not performing when he is on the other side of the church door during the performance. He is reminding the audience that they are all poets.

Grief is the vase found in between the outlines of literature and religion. Nonhuman primates grieve. Apes and monkeys can grieve for the loss of life due to the loss of habitat. The primate uses his ferocious energy to enhance the cuteness of the stuffed animal primates through comparison to himself. He is showing us that he is very powerful. He shows us how humans have commodified primates and made them cute. In this case, cuteness is synonymous with stillness. The power of movement and martial arts is not available to the stuffed primates except through Fowler's behavior. He is illustrating the hierarchical relationship between humanity and other primates. The nonhuman primates are helpless against humans altering their habitat. Ngai writes:

> Cuteness is a way of aestheticizing powerlessness. It hinges on a sentimental attitude toward the diminutive and/or weak, which is why cute objects—formally simple or noncomplex,

---

9. SJ Fowler, 'About Poem Brut', *Poem Brut*, <https://www.poembrut.com> [accessed 10th May 2022]

and deeply associated with the infantile, the feminine, and the unthreatening—get even cuter when perceived as injured or disabled. So there's a sadistic side to this tender emotion.[10]

By enacting a monkey in a church Fowler is asking the audience to accept a measure of indignity in the house of god. He is asking how we might feel if monkeys treated our habitat the way we treat theirs? The stuffed animal primates are present to mitigate the christian outrage with their cuteness. Here is an example of deliberately deploying cuteness to tone down the physical intensity at play.

Literature is the vase found in between the outlines of birth and evolution. Fowler tells the audience that he is concerned with the dignity of the poet; then, he spends the rest of the performance imitating great apes and monkeys. This might be seen as making his former statement ironic. Or it might be seen as completing his former statement with the concept of employing the dignity of the poet to illustrate the dignity of the great apes. The origin of dignity is worth. The primate in all his ambiguity is insisting that the great apes are a worthy subject for poetry; he is preaching to the audience.

Evolution is the vase found in between the outlines of literature and religion. The great apes enter the poetry reading and the church to save us outsiders trapped inside this traditional location. They give us the evolution of humanity. The presence of the different species of great apes serves as a mirror for the different human faiths present at St John's on Bethnal Green. They ask us to expand our sympathies and reduce our sense of self-importance. The great apes tell us that if we can not see their humanity, then we are smaller than we thought ourselves before the performance. The apes have gathered here to celebrate, to tell us that poetry is itself a great lake – it is deep and the tides are dangerous and it holds a reservoir of fresh water that will save us all. The subject of the performance is the space in between great apes and the anglican faith. The great apes are here to reflect our humanity back to us; they are here to stand beside us and let us admire the reflected breadth of poetry.

Literature is the vase found in between the outlines of evolution and grief. This is not the first performance Fowler has given for the love of a forest, high erratic ecology, and its vulnerability. He performed with Kiwan Sung at Beyond Words: South Korean & British poets in collaboration – Rich Mix : June Saturday 3rd 2017, where they illustrated the relationship between a bear and a tree.[11] Julia Rose Lewis responded to this performance in a creative critical haibun in her poetry collection High Erratic Ecology. She wrote:

---

10. Sianne Ngai, 'OUR AESTHETIC CATEGORIES: AN INTERVIEW WITH SIANNE NGAI', (interviewed by Adam Jasper for Cabinet, Fall 2011, Forensics) [2011] < https://www.cabinetmagazine.org/issues/43/jasper_ngai.php> [accessed 12th April 2022]

11. SJ Fowler, 'Beyond Words: South Korean & British poets in collaboration - Rich Mix : June Saturday 3rd 2017', *Enemies Project* <http://www.theenemiesproject.com/southkorea> [accessed 15th May 2022]

Roots present the bear with a chair and the bear seats himself. What are eyes but blemishes in the skin? Blue him wishes into the holes in the tree trunk, they are eye to eye. The branches of the tree grow in the direction of the bear as the bear leans into the trunk of the tree. They come eye to eye again as if they could listen to their blemished wishes, as if symmetry is enough to make things come true.[12]

The symmetry lies in mutual need between the bear and tree. The bear is a creature of the forest – as is the orangutan. The species name means 'forest person' in Malay. The orangutan brings his love affair with the forest into the church with him. This is hieratic ecology; the relationship between primates and trees.

Grief is the vase found in between the outlines of evolution and literature. The scene in which Fowler lays under the rug with the stuffed animal primate on top of the rug on top of him. The poetics of scale here illustrate a larger rug, a smaller human, and a tiny stuffed animal primate. If the stillness of Fowler is seen as death, then the rug turns into blanket of dirt, and the stuffed animal primate is a sign and gravestone marking the extinction of nonhuman primates. Cuteness is sitting on extinction. Poetry about the sixth great extinction can not let itself become taxidermy.

---

12. Julia Rose Lewis, *High Erratic Ecology* (Newton-le-Willows: Knives Forks and Spoons Press, 2020)

Works Cited

Bachelard, Gaston, *Poetics of Space*, trans. Maria Jolas (Boston, MA: Beacon Press, 1994)

Broken Sleep Books, 'SJ Fowler - The Great Apes', *Broken Sleep Books*, 30 April 2022 <https://www.brokensleepbooks.com/product-page/sj-fowler-the-great-apes> [accessed 1st May 2022]

Filevich, Elisa et al. 'Seeing Double: Exploring the Phenomenology of Self-Reported Absence of Rivalry in Bistable Pictures', *Frontiers in human neuroscience* vol. 11 301, 9th June 2017, doi:10.3389

Fowler, SJ, 'About Poem Brut', *Poem Brut*, <https://www.poembrut.com> [accessed 10th May 2022]

Fowler, SJ, *A Note on Launching Great Apes By Being an Ape*, <https://steven-fowler-1pys.squarespace.com/blog/2022/4/13/a-note-on-launching-great-apes-by-being-an-ape> [accessed 10th April 2022]

Fowler, SJ, 'Beyond Words: South Korean & British poets in collaboration - Rich Mix : June Saturday 3rd 2017', *Enemies Project* <http://www.theenemiesproject.com/southkorea> [accessed 15th May 2022]

Fowler, SJ, *The Great Apes*, online video recording, YouTube, 7th April 2022, <https://www.youtube.com/watch?v=RtvyEdlG5ec> [accessed 12th April 2022]

Grobstein, Paul, 'Getting It Less Wrong, The Brain's Way: Science, Pragmatism, and Multiplism', *INTERPRETATION AND ITS OBJECTS: Studies in the Philosophy of Michael Krausz*, ed. by Andreea Deciu Ritivoi (New York, New York: Rodopi, 2003)

Jane Goodall Institute, 'PROJECT ISSUE: WILDLIFE TRAFFICKING & ILLEGAL TRADE', *Jane Goodall Institute*, <https://www.janegoodall.org/wildlife-trafficking-trade/> [accessed 15th April 2022]

Lewis, Julia Rose, *High Erratic Ecology* (Newton-le-Willows: Knives Forks and Spoons Press, 2020)

Ngai, Sianne, 'OUR AESTHETIC CATEGORIES: AN INTERVIEW WITH SIANNE NGAI', (interviewed by Adam Jasper for *Cabinet*, Fall 2011, Forensics) [2011] < https://www.cabinetmagazine.org/issues/43/jasper_ngai.php> [accessed 12th April 2022]

Editors of the Oxford English Dictionary, 'Primate', *Oxford English Dictionary*, <https://www.oed.com/dictionary/primate_n1?tab=meaning_and_use#28339980> [accessed 2nd May 2022]

Elaborate Biological Filigrees

History is blindness to all that you are going to say to me soon.[1]

SJ Fowler is inquiring what chimpanzees have to say about our blindness to our life history? It is a mirror not a miracle. Haeckel's Law states that ontogeny recapitulates phylogeny. Ontogeny refers to the unfolding of the body of the organism in time otherwise known as embryology and developmental biology. Without it, we synthesize again and again and soon we are lost. Haeckel writes: 'we do not really understand [the facts of embryology] until we trace them to their true phylogenetic causes, and see that each of these apparently simple processes is the recapitulation of a long series of *historical* changes'.[2] Phylogeny refers to the unrolling of species in time otherwise known as descent with modification and evolutionary biology.

The origin of recapitulation means gone through heading by heading, chapter repeating, again diminutive of head. Let us go through the series of readings. Fowler created a film reading of *The Great Apes* for the Broken Sleep Books Extravaganza on 14th April 2022.[3][4] The event took place after the face-to-face launch of *The Great Apes* and before the online launch.[5][6]

The reading unrolls a life history of violence, sex, and loneliness. To read is to masquerade. To read is to filter and reveal oneself through the selection of a mask. Before the chimpanzee he wore a mask to make his half-face into a skull. He is illustrating the skill of living in the divide between

---

1. Ghazal Mosadeq, 'a diagnostic ophthalmic treatise for the ob oculus', *Blackbox Manifold*, summer 2021, <http://www.manifold.group.shef.ac.uk/issue26/index26.html> [accessed 19th April 2022].
2. Stephen Jay Gould is quoting and Earnst Haeckel translated into English. Stephen Jay Gould, *Ontogeny and Phylogeny*, (London: The Belknap Press of Harvard University Press, 1977) p. 193.
3. SJ Fowler, *The Great Apes*, (Rhydwen, Wales: Broken Sleep Books, 2022)
4. *Broken Sleep Books Extravaganza Part 2*, dir. Aaron Kent (Broken Sleep Books 2022)
5. SJ Fowler, *Orangutan*, online video recording, YouTube, 1st May 2022, <https://www.youtube.com/watch?v=GWaHHDaRzUc> [accessed 10th May 2022].
6. SJ Fowler, *The Great Apes*, online video recording, YouTube, 7th April 2022, <https://www.youtube.com/watch?v=RtvyEdlG5ec> [accessed 25th May 2022].

birth and the inevitable unfolding toward death; his eyes are alive and his mouth is only bone. It is important to note the similarities between our reading and Fowler's collaboration with with Icelandic poet Ásta Fanney Sigurðardóttir in a performance at the Rich Mix Arts Centre for the European Poetry Night 2017.[7] The performance begins in awkwardness and ends with explicitly defying social conventions well beyond the poetry reading. Their collaboration explores consumption, death, motherhood, and respect. The development, the unfolding of an experimental poet's body of work recapitulates the evolution of literary forms. Haeckel's Law obtains with respect to experimental poetry.

Phylogeny unfolds the self. Paleontologist Stephen Jay Gould writes 'phylogeny unfolds historically as the sequence of ontogenies for all organisms making up a lineage'.[8] Fowler is looking through the eyes of a chimpanzee mask, because it is one of the organisms that makes up his lineage. He is illustrating his own phylogeny in *The Great Apes*. He is looking into the ways in which his own life history extends before birth and after grief. There is violence, sex, and loneliness unfolding before the chimp face that he has placed facing the audience. These ironies he reveals are given to the reader to revel in themselves.

Ontogeny unrolls the self. Fowler is unrolling line after line of the chimpanzee poem. He repeats the phrase, it's a fight, twice in the reading and its echoing creates a stillness in sound and meaning following itself. It's a fight that's so still to refrigerator, where the fight is a long unresolved conflict, where the fight is decay slowed to the point of stillness as a refrigerator slows the growth of bacteria and mold. Is he saying refrigerator or refrigerate her, where refrigerate means to hold her body before burial, the reader finds themselves in the middle of grief. Is the fight consuming her or foreshadowing 'Mary mother of glitter' in the next line?[9] In the supermarket, it is a fight with consumerism and modernity. Here refrigerate comes from back cold becoming; it is the exposure of the private time in the public. So the supermarket is recalling the human missing the chimp part of himself. There is primate echoing private. Chimps have thick hair down their backs that helps them maintain body temperature in cold and rain and it is missing from humans. Ontogeny unrolls; it is the vase found before the outlines of birth and grief.

Fowler is illustrating the literature of phylogeny by unfolding himself. There is glitter in his eyes. It is the refection of the reflection that is shining inside him and outside. The mask castes his eyes into shadow and hides the rest of his face making his expression different to read. The genetic code is

---

7. SJ Fowler and Ásta Fanney Sigurðardóttir, *European Poetry Night 2017*, online video recording, YouTube, 7th May 2017, <https://www.youtube.com/watch?v=-YIK3WPD6iM> [accessed 25th May 2022].
8. Stephen Jay Gould, *Ontogeny and Phylogeny*, p. 212.
9. SJ Fowler, *The Great Apes*, p.19.

also glittering inside the offspring. David Spittle illuminates the relationship between a life history and glitter. He writes:

> we glitter. gravel. grave. as brains. abrade. unmade.[10]

We are glitter brains, we litter our grey matter all over the planet, we describe our brains as bright, not unlike glitter, he catches a glimmer of himself in the glitter and flickering light of the monitor. Gravel abrades, it slows, it sloughs off larger rocks or boulders, it is greater than glitter, it is used in construction (especially landscapes), it is something small that humans form. Graves are the unmaking of humans, the place where decomposition takes place. Graves are possibly where the gravestone will turn to gravel. Glitter causes cancer and cancer is what grows into gravel, abrading our bodies, it is killing and filling out graves. We are made as we are unmade in evolutionary-developmental biology.

Developmental biology is the vase found before the outlines of birth and grief. So to write, as Fowler does, that one is 'alone and crying folds into ropes' is to say that when ejaculating by oneself, the sperm does not lead to the development of an embryo.[11] These ropes are a metaphor for the deoxyribonucleic acid contained in sperm. The ropes echoing hopes opposite being along and crying. What is orgasm a metaphor for? To fold is the necessary opposite of unfolding and developmental biology. To fold is closing down. Cells fold down in apoptosis, which is essential to development and not developing cancer. Fowler elaborates this paradox, 'and cigarettes are wanted in my mouth despite the / aforementioned cancer'.[12] Humans want that which they know will kill them and make it available to themselves in modern supermarkets. It is this kind of knowing that makes and unmakes humans.

Violence unrolls. Is it the limbs or the mind that revels in violence? Where is it that violence unfolds from the proximal to the distal, from the mind to the limbs. The limbs themselves might be as lambs or lamb sausage. Fowler raises the question that violence might be a human construct, that it might be the thing that separates us from the great apes. Perhaps for apes there is only predation, sex, and territoriality. Violence gives; it finds humanity a sense of drive; it is the foundation and filigree of modernity. It is fine ornamental work all the way down. Humans need a concept of violence to lend themselves an understanding of death. Violence resides inside the human mind.

The foundation for the body unfolds in time. The subject of the poem follows the head to the foot, tongue to limb, hourglass overturning itself.

---

10. David Spittle, 'glitter gravel grave', *Rubbles*, (Rhydwen, Wales: Broken Sleep Books, 2022) p.9.
11. SJ Fowler, *The Great Apes*, p.20.
12. ibid.

Tongue as the style or manner of speaking, as a reflection of where one is coming from, a particular language, the tongue of a shoe, a long low promontory of land. It is the inferior-superior axis in developmental biology, a fine line feet to head, that is perfectly reversed in a headstand. Fowler is turning over the question of superiority; is it chimp to human or human to chimp? He is turning over violence and knowledge again and gain like an hourglass; he leaves the reader with only a fine line of sand to mark the following time.

The reading unrolls the filigree from seed and thread; it is a roll of film falling open for the audience. It is a narrative full of sexual references, not only for the sake of companionship and orgasm, for the love of evolutionary-developmental biology. Fowler refers to a pair of apes and indicates a parental lineage for a human extending all the way back to the chimps. He writes, 'with limps on both apes until they become limbs'.[13] The ape pair is a reference to parental dependence during early life, specifically in the time before humans are bipedal. The ape pair refers to human forearms employed in quadrupedal locomotion. To become human in patterns of movement is as much about bipedal locomotion as it is becoming sexually mature.

Meaning is what we unfold. The filigree recapitulates the foundation life after life. Fowler reveals that the unrolling of literature recapitulates the unfolding of the poet. He revels in the irony given our life history. He writes:

> Humour is essentially self-mocking derision, and all
> Freudian humour is replete with unhappy black bile,
> melancholia ... How much sillier could it be that we are
> sentient apes who know we are alive and know we will die
> and are able to perceive enough to know we don't know
> much and must strive for meaning anyway.[14]

Literature is this aliveness to human striving for meaning; it is the life of filigrees. History is blindness to all that will unroll from ourselves, to synthesize again and again and soon we are lost; we will have lost sight of evolution. What Fowler puts into relief is that poetry and literature is the same foundational story of all organisms: birth, growth, occasional companionship (read sex), occasional joy/exaltation (read orgasm), more isolation, decay, and death. He has deconstructed very deeply our history to remind us all of our common origin, but don't forget we all fall unique one of a kind as well. The filigrees unrolled by each human in aggregate is our uniqueness in phylogenetic space.

---

13. ibid.
14. James Knight, 'Interview with SJ Fowler', *Steel Incisors*, 31st July 2021 <https://www.steelincisors.com/s/stories/bastard-poems> [Accessed 12th May 2022].

Works Cited:

Broken Sleep Books Extravaganza Part 2, dir. Aaron Kent (Broken Sleep Books 2022)

Fowler, SJ, *The Great Apes,* (Rhydwen, Wales: Broken Sleep Books, 2022)

Fowler, SJ, *The Great Apes,* online video recording, YouTube, 7 April 2022, <https://www.youtube.com/watch?v=RtvyEdlG5ec> [accessed 25 May 2022]

Fowler, SJ, *Orangutan,* online video recording, YouTube, 1 May 2022, <https://www.youtube.com/watch?v=GWaHHDaRzUc> [accessed 10 May 2022]

Fowler, SJ and Sigurðardóttir, Ásta Fanney, *European Poetry Night 2017,* online video recording, YouTube, 7 May 2017, <https://www.youtube.com/watch?v=-YIK3WPD6iM> [accessed 25 May 2022]

Gould, Stephen Jay, *Ontogeny and Phylogeny,* (London: The Belknap Press of Harvard University Press, 1977)

Knight, James, 'Interview with SJ Fowler', *Steel Incisors,* 31st July 2021 <https://www.steelincisors.com/s/stories/bastard-poems> [Accessed 12th May 2022]

Mosadeq, Ghazal, 'a diagnostic ophthalmic treatise for the ob oculus', *Blackbox Manifold,* summer 2021, <http://www.manifold.group.shef.ac.uk/issue26/index26.html> [accessed 19 April 2022]

Spittle, David, 'glitter gravel grave', *Rubbles,* (Rhydwen, Wales: Broken Sleep Books, 2022)

Can an orangutan be too shrewd?

Ambiguity gives birth to poetry. Birth is the vase found in between the outlines of evolution and literature. The poem, 'Orangutan' had its first birthday party at the Broken Sleep Books event at St John's on Bethnal Green 7th April 2022.[1] The second birthday was the Broken Sleep Books online launch 30th April 2022.[2] Let us watch back in the sense to guard intensively. The orangutan is following the bonobo and anticipating the human form in *The Great Apes*.[3] If the film poem is not only a facet of the physical performance, then we have our exploration unrolling the body of SJ Fowler's work before us.

Orangutan is the vase found in between the outlines of film and poem. As a face-vase ambiguous figure, *Orangutan* can be seen in three ways: as a face reflected to itself, as a vase, and as both a face and a vase. It is a film mirroring a poem imperfectly as a pond might do. *Orangutan* is intense curiosity held inside a glass vessel, and it is relentless as a satire of intellectualism. It is a film commenting on the performance of a poem to make material an open-ended inquiry into the relationship between the frog brain and the storyteller. Evolution is the vase found in between the outlines of birth and religion.

Birth is the vase found in between the outlines of evolution and religion. Evolution is the vase found in between the outlines of birth and literature. Literature is the vase found in between the outlines of birth and grief. Grief is the vase found in between the outlines of evolution and religion. Religion is the vase found in between the outlines of birth and literature. Literature is the vase found in between the outlines of evolution and religion. Religion is the vase found in between the outlines of birth and grief. Grief is the vase

---

1. SJ Fowler, *The Great Apes*, online video recording, YouTube, 7th April 2022, <https://www.youtube.com/watch?v=RtvyEdlG5ec> [accessed 25th May 2022].
2. SJ Fowler, *Orangutan*, online video recording, YouTube, 1st May 2022, <https://www.youtube.com/watch?v=GWaHHDaRzUc> [accessed 10th May 2022].
3. SJ Fowler, *The Great Apes*, (Rhydwen, Wales: Broken Sleep Books, 2022).

found in between the outlines of birth and evolution. Birth is the vase found in between the outlines of grief and literature. Literature is the vase found in the between the outlines of birth and religion. Religion is the vase found in between the outlines of evolution and literature. Evolution is the vase found in between the outlines of birth and grief. Grief is the vase found in between the outlines of literature and religion. Literature is the vase found in between the outlines of birth and evolution. Evolution is the vase found in between the outlines of literature and religion. Literature is the vase found in between the outlines of evolution and grief. Grief is the vase found in between the outlines of evolution and literature.

London is unrolling itself. Evolution is the vase found in between the outlines of grief and literature. Fowler and Joshua Alexander explore the ways in which the city's unrolling effects a new definition of grief itself in literature. Their film poem, *Animal Drums*, premiered at Whitechapel Gallery, London in 2019. They play with ambiguity to foreground the city and background its inhabitants. Fowler writes:

> London disappears under the ground of the film's ambiguous protagonist, who is half victim, half perpetrator. Gently mad, positively lost, we follow our host through the bounds of a changing, money-washed capital city.[4]

The film poem gives the audience a human face and a figure in the city to follow and facilitates switching between seeing the face, figure, and both. The film is unfolding to follow the face of the protagonist as a metaphor for London being the face of the country.

Grief is the vase found in between the outlines of birth and religion. Grief is the result of loving a place. It is the twin of relief of disappearing into the background of fitting into place. Fowler reads:

> stupidly profound, exciting sensation, touching immediately on the self, that one had when sniffing at one's own skin[5]

Here is an inquiry into the nature of privacy. Where is one free to explore the self, its sensations, its sense of ownership over those sensations is the body of the problem. There is no privacy for the primate without its own environment. Fowler is asking what the primate knows about deforestation, climate change, and humanity. Do primates worships humans as humans worship themselves? What does it does it mean when a human begins to

---

4. SJ Fowler, 'ANIMAL DRUMS, Joshua ALEXANDER & SJ FOWLER' *Partisan Hotel*, <https://partisanhotel.co.uk/Animal-Drums> [accessed 12th June 2022].

5. *Orangutan*, 9:27.

worship a nonhuman primate to elevate an orangutan? The film poem shows nonhuman primates existing in human environments by means of overlaying footage and faces to fade away.

Birth is the vase found in between the outlines of evolution and literature. Fowler is driven by the orangutan. His face is first overlayed with the steering wheel, the forearms, and finally the face of the great ape. The orangutan is turned into his lens for interpreting humanity. It is only by moving closer to the orangutan that he can become himself more willfully human. The orangutan has been with Fowler since his birth, because it is a part of his evolutionary-developmental history, like a sibling. Fowler has been with the orangutan since the first word of the first poem, since he found a publisher for the collection, since the launch, and now the film poem of the launch. The film poem *Orangutan* is the vase found in between the outlines of Fowler and an actual orangutan. He is suggesting that if we travel back along this evolutionary lineage to a distant past existence, then we will find the mirror of ourselves in our movements.

Literature is the vase found in between the outlines of birth and religion. It is the lines repeating to give form to the body and the words; for the love of language, it is repetition that gives the pattern. Lines connect humans to the minds of themselves and other animals. The collision of the human mind with a solid line can lead to a concussion, and repeated concussions can lead to CTE.[6] The diagnosis of chronic traumatic encephalopathy is doubtful before grief. It is a life history told to a doctor. It is a disease that takes account of the accumulations of a human lifetime. Fowler writes:

> brain damage
> cte disconnecting[7]

These lines interrupt the repetition at the beginning of the four previous lines and the following page. The anaphora is gesturing at the process of aging, unfolding in time, and a steady decline that begins with birth and heads toward the grief of others. The film poem is marking a lifetime with the twins as growth and grief meeting again and again. Two shaken lines taken together give the outline of a vase or a pair of faces and make to shake together the brain like a shellfish.

The human mind is the vessel found in between the outlines of birth and religion. The faces outline the shell following the mind. There fall lines drawn by a shaking hand, a trembling hand, the line reflects the state of the brain. The vase and two faces ambiguous figure is driving at a concussion at the brain seeing what it has done to the brain, it is a reckoning and a

---

6. National Health Service, 'Chronic Traumatic Encephalopathy' *Health A-Z*, 17th April 2022 <https://www.nhs.uk/conditions/chronic-traumatic-encephalopathy/> [accessed 6th June 2022].

7. *Orangutan*, 5:56.

making room for grief in literature. To shake violently or violently shaken is hinting to seizures that often follow severe concussions.[8] The origin of concussion is to dash together to shake. To dash the brain to the ground and to shake the brain inside the skull. The vase is liquid glass before it is shattered, before there are shards and sharps to be collected. The origin of the word ambiguous is to drive both ways, to drive one's interpretation both ways is perceiving the faces and the vase.[9] Ambiguous in the sense indistinct, obscure, doubtful, wavering, going around both ways to drive. To go driving around like the orangutan in the film. The forest person is not in the forest first and is not acting like themselves second. This brain disconnect is one reason for the doubling of faces other than the obvious seeing double as a symptom.[10]

Birth is the vase found in between the outlines of grief and religion. The human mind is thinking of the liquid found in between the outlines of bone and orangutan. It comes after asking us the audience to buy the book, to take the book home. To see double is to see the faces and not the vase as the figure. To see double is telling us something about the nature of glass, because old glassware does not bounce, it breaks. That is to say that vases are not unlike brains, they can only be dropped some many times in a lifetime. To see double is to see oneself in another light, mirror, or film. The book might embody some trauma. The book might be making or masking some trauma, but it is certainly not autobiographical. He holds *The Great Apes* in front of his face like a mask, like the orangutan in the film overlay to say that there is always something between him and the audience. The reading ends with Fowler hitting his head against the book over and over again.

Religion is the vase found in between the outlines of birth and evolution. There is a role for religion in the stories of evolution and the evolution of stories as told by groups of overly-verbal great apes. It is a human narrative told to help make sense of our life history. It is primates all the way down, because the orangutan is not unlike the ascetics living in the forest. In Siddhartha, his novel on Buddhism, Herman Hesse writes:

> You know, my friend, that even as a young man, when we lived with the ascetics in the forest, I came to distrust doctrines and teachers and to turn my back on them.[11]

---

8. Editors of the Oxford English Dictionary, 'Concussion', *Oxford English Dictionary*, <https://www.oed.com/dictionary/primate_n1?tab=meaning_and_use#28339980> [accessed 2nd May 2022]
9. Editors of the Oxford English Dictionary, 'Ambiguous', Oxford English Dictionary, <https://www.oed.com/dictionary/ambiguous_adj?tab=etymology#5545590> [accessed 16th June 2022].
10. National Health Service, 'Chronic Traumatic Encephalopathy'.
11. Herman Hesse, *Siddhartha* (Mineola, New York: Dover Publications, 1998)

Fowler is suggesting it is only human to let our overly verbal intellect tell us stories and in turn to criticize those stories. He writes, 'a big red spoiled brat done good like buddha'.[12] Here he is deflecting with some humor. Fowler is elucidating a parallel between evolutionary biology and religious learning; it is narratives of human intellect all the way down. *The Great Apes* is a narrative of what can be learned by living in the forest with other primates. Storytelling is the birthright of overly verbal apes. The orangutan is the background whispering to the foregrounded human nature. It is the vase found in between the outlines of literature and religion. Fowler reads:

> the big boy
> is overhead all apart from love
> orangutan won't fight, say what you like
> it won't be had
> a wingspan stands before insult
> though orangutan whispers to his followers
> monkeys, dogs, frogs[13]

When he reads the last line the steering wheel is laying over his lips giving a sense of human drives, a sense of negation in a thick black line, and a sense of physical limits to language as he reads the word whispers. Here is a narrative of ape to overly verbal ape perception; the human is a fellow, not a follower of the orangutan. If literature and religion are facets of storytelling then it is not a diminutive of face, but a feature of human nature being revealed.

Birth is the vase found in between the outlines of literature and religion. Birth is itself repetition of the species. It is a measure of their overall health and survival, so overly verbal apes have created extensive lists of the repetition of births in species in order to study ecology. The International Union for Conservation of Nature publishes a red list of threatened species.[14] In reading the biological literature, so the red list becomes the past tense to fast forward into a litany of losses we know we must face. It is important to note the orangutan exits in the space where yellow wishes red. Fowler reads:

> what you seek
> deforestation as a metaphor for death itself
> the kind of creature who invents the word being confused
> for the sensation of being stumped[15]

---

12. SJ Fowler, *The Great Apes*, p.84.
13. *Orangutan*, 2:16.
14. International Union for Conservation of Nature, 'Orangutan', *IUCN Red List of Threatened Species*, 2022 <https://www.iucnredlist.org/search?query=orangutan&searchType=species> [accessed 1st July 2022].
15. *Orangutan*, 2:54.

Deforestation is a recipe for the death of the orangutan. In this ambiguous figure, there can be no orangutan without the forest background. Fowler reveals the orangutan is the figure. Survival is the vase found in between the outlines of the orangutan and the human. Fowler is relocating the orangutan in relationship to himself in order to show that the death of the orangutan is a metaphor for the great apes – including humanity. Reading is returning to literary history as the orangutan is revisiting evolutionary history. The very act of driving gives us a sense of power and ownership that Fowler wants to criticize in the film poem by means of the ridiculous.

Fowler reveals his own red list as a parallel between an aging overly verbal ape and a planet suffering the ravages of climate change. Religion is the vase found in between the outlines of grief and literature. Intellectualism is its own religion. Here he is inquiring into the balance between life history and loss. He reads:

> a big red understanding after soaked experience
> a big red keeping itself to itself steeped in books
> a big red onion anti-moan
> o professeur[16]

To be named and known as professor recognizes the highest intellectual achievements and reinforces the high erratic ecosystem of postmodernism. However, the last line in the list is a negation of its own sound and sense. It is the bad taste left between grief and literature. A red sun is setting or rising, either is romantic, and the onion is the opposite of romantic. Here is a foil for the sun, for staring at the sun which refers to death, and the little death refers to orgasm by means of another anatomy. It is only nostalgia that fetishizes philosophy for the love of wisdom. Fowler refers to the human need to interpret, indeed, he might be redefining religion as the human need to worship intellectual work.

Satire is the vase found in between the outlines of grief and literature. Here is where the pleasure of intellectualizing and the intellectualizing of pleasure falls. Otherwise known as overly verbal apes fall down. Fowler is inquiring into the role of naming as a way of knowing what language can give. He names and renames the orangutan to foreground the role of sound and background the role of meaning in verbal language. He is hinting to the failures of overly verbal apes by introducing the music of Henry Flynt simultaneously with the image of the orangutan driving the vehicle.[17] The orangutan driving the vehicle is a comment on the nature of the metaphor, the

---

16. ibid., 3:45.
17. ibid., 2:21. Henry Flynt, *Purified by Fire*, YouTube 9th April 2016 <https://www.youtube.com/watch?v=Cnma2Q2QHGI> [accessed 2nd July 2022].

vehicle is the human invention that is carrying over the utterly unknowable orangutan, who becomes by the end of the film poem, the known unknown.

Grief is the vase found in between the outlines of birth and literature. Grief is found in the manuscript. This is the writing before the book becomes public literature. Here is the unknown known danger, where reading leads to archaeology, biology, and geology of knowledge. It is the subject of the H.P. Lovecraft novella, *At the Mountains of Madness*, and more. If following the web of references, let us go further back to *The Narrative of Arthur Gordon Pym of Nantucket* by Edgar Allen Poe and then forward to *Moby Dick* by Herman Melville and *Star Trek IV: The Voyage Home* directed by Leonard Nimoy. This intellectual lineage is concerned with the dangers of knowing too little and too much about ancient monsters otherwise known as whales. In the sound the word innocent holds the homonym for knowledge and its negation. In the sense the word innocent means not harming. Fowler reads:

> there is another country where one is at home, where
> everything one does is innocent.[18]

Home might be better known as a question of intentionality. He reads this part in the film poem completely masked with the black and blue and clothing and ocean and sky and train. Horror is that the figure can disappear into the ground.

Birth is the vase found in between the outlines of evolution and grief. Even overly verbal apes are born with a frog brain. The frog brain means the cognitive unconscious, multitasking, and specialized skills. The frog brain is responsible for reacting to the world outside. The storyteller reacts to the frog brain reacting and explains why it behaves the way it does. The storyteller or neocortex gives the internal experience of agency, analysis, ideals, imagination, free will, thinking, and thinking about thinking. *Orangutan* gives a narrative about thinking and thinking about thinking. Fowler reading in the room fades to Fowler in the church worshipping the orangutan stuffed animal in the moment he reads the word abreacting.[19] The film poem simultaneously is showing and telling; it is striving to drive away the first reaction. It is the storyteller reacting to the reaction of the frog brain.

Evolution is the vase found in between the outlines of grief and religion. Fact to fiction to nonfiction to cut nature at the joint. Evolution has a history that will unroll itself like a ball of string and we can follow after the fact. There is a moment in the film poem where the hand of the orangutan on the steering wheel is larger than its head and only the human head is larger yet.

---

18. *Orangutan*, 9:44.
19. ibid., 5:21

Can an orangutan be too shrewd?

Here is the storytelling human in the middle of things. There is the silent frog brain that mediates the experience of language for the storyteller. It is interpretation all the way down. Evolution is only a line given in the unrolling of a ball of string and extinction is the ball running out. The human poem is the beginning of the end. *Orangutan* illustrates the ways in which overly verbal apes take evolution and literature for their religion. Religion is the vase found in between the outlines of evolution and grief.

28 Wilfred Franklin & Julia Rose Lewis

Works Cited

Henry Flynt, *Purified by Fire*, YouTube 9 April 2016 <https://www.youtube.com/watch?v=Cnma2Q2QHGI> [accessed 2nd July 2022]

SJ Fowler, 'ANIMAL DRUMS, Joshua ALEXANDER & SJ FOWLER' *Partisan Hotel*, <https://partisanhotel.co.uk/Animal-Drums> [accessed 12th June 2022]

SJ Fowler, *The Great Apes*, (Rhydwen, Wales: Broken Sleep Books, 2022)

SJ Fowler, *The Great Apes*, online video recording, YouTube, 7th April 2022, <https://www.youtube.com/watch?v=RtvyEdlG5ec> [accessed 25th May 2022]

SJ Fowler, *Orangutan*, online video recording, YouTube, 1st May 2022, <https://www.youtube.com/watch?v=GWaHHDaRzUc> [accessed 10th May 2022]

Herman Hesse, *Siddhartha* (Mineola, New York: Dover Publications, 1998)

International Union for Conservation of Nature, 'Orangutan', *IUCN Red List of Threatened Species*, 2022 <https://www.iucnredlist.org/search?query=orangutan&searchType=species> [accessed 1st July 2022]

Editors of the Oxford English Dictionary, 'Ambiguous', Oxford English Dictionary, <https://www.oed.com/dictionary/ambiguous_adj?tab=etymology#5545590> [accessed 16th June 2022]

Editors of the *Oxford English Dictionary*, 'Concussion', *Oxford English Dictionary*, <https://www.oed.com/dictionary/primate_n1?tab=meaning_and_use#28339980> [accessed 2nd May 2022]

National Health Service, 'Chronic Traumatic Encephalopathy' *Health A-Z*, 17th April 2022 <https://www.nhs.uk/conditions/chronic-traumatic-encephalopathy/> [accessed 6th June 2022]

If Fulfilling Then Family

The human poem is telling the story of the great ape family. It looks backward. Humans are the youngest and yet the longest lived in the hominid family. For Fowler, the family tree is a forest in fact, the place for us to rest and reassure ourselves that we have a place in the world. He wants humans to look beyond biography for the love of understanding. The unfolding of a lifetime is familiar. The study of development itself needs ecology and evolution in order to make sense. *The Great Apes*[1] lays out different facets of humanity as siblings often weather in the same way from the same experiences and environment. To be both the youngest and the longest living means loneliness, loss, and a sudden need to listen closely to humankind.

Fowler makes the familiar unfolding of a lifetime foreign by looking further back to the beginning of species. Further is the far side for animal limbs, more remote, and late in the day. Further before is a far distant ancestor. The first ape to stand and make use of bipedal locomotion foremost. The *human* poem begins with:

> a mystery
> on the ape's face
> as it limped from the primordial
> juice
> was resurrection
> restlessness
> a story about a story[2]

Here is the oldest identified. The first of the mostly vertical apes is foreshadowing old age. Life history is a story of a story. Humanity manifests its restlessness as a retelling of this story. It is the head and the mind inside is held higher then and overshadows the quadrupedal apes in the story

---

1. SJ Fowler, *The Great Apes*, (Rhydwen, Wales: Broken Sleep Books, 2022)
2. ibid,, p.99.

telling. There is the human need to understand stories all the way down. The human need to tell stories to intellectualize to revitalize life and to throw ever greater shadows over the world to hold it.

This is the story of the overly verbal and overly vertical apes. It prepositions humanity. The narrative equates verbal and vertical with one another. There is the relentless need to tell stories that position humanity head and shoulders above the great apes. Fowler is relentless in his interrogation of this simple placement. He reads the recent advances in anthropology and biology into the stories humans tell about themselves. Dalke and Grobstein write on interdisciplinarity:

> The grist for scientific inquiry emerges from story-
> comparing; the products of science in turn become a part of
> the comparative story-telling that fuels the humanities.[3]

Hear the evolution of stories and the stories of evolution interacting in real time. As stories of evolutionary and developmental biology begin to humble humanity, so the evolving stories we tell must also reflect this new humility. This willingness to hold humanity in a lower and wider position inside the three dimensional world is wild. It is this complex placement that Fowler explores in the human poem.

The human poem is unraveling the narrative. Far and near the great apes need humanity to help them forward. It revisits its own once and future commitments and reconstitutes its journey from naive to knowing. The old distance between apes and overly verbal apes is lost. The human poem is making the point that we are, right now, the youngest oldest siblings in the Hominid family. Fowler writes:

> a nice juicy bone
> was to be had
> was the gleam of the city
> was civil ise[4]

Civil eyes. The eyes are the subject looking backwards. The lyric first person singular that is looking back at past tense formulations of the verb 'to be', literally, back words. 'Was to be' is infinitely wistful, and yet, to be had means to have been made a fool or otherwise tricked. Old needs once

---

3. Anne Dalke and Paul Grobstein, 'Three-Dimensional Story Telling: An Exploration of Teaching Reading, Writing, and Beyond', *Journal of Teaching Writing*. 2007 <https://serendipstudio.org/~pgrobste/pdfs/3DStoryTelling07.pdf> [accessed 10th August 2022] p.110.

4. SJ Fowler, *The Great Apes*, p.100.

upon a time were met and not forever more. It is a discovery revealed in the difference between evolutionary time and a human lifetime.

In order to continue unrolling the story of the great apes, it is time for humans to care for these similar beings. Humanity has had the privilege of being the youngest siblings in the family. To be self-referential to the point of selfishness. It is the very privilege of humanity that means there needs to be a role reversal. It is first the elongated lifespan. It is pairing the newest with the longest also known as the surest loneliness. It is second the explosion in population numbers. It is the relative decline in the great apes population that humans need to attend. Far and wide the effects of climate change have been felt, will continue to be felt, and will accelerate the decrease in the great ape population. The old distance between the apes and the overly verbal apes will grow until the time humanity is left alone with itself. Fowler illustrates this loss and loneliness by means of kinship.

It is a question of how kin and kindness unfold. The human poem inquires into the relationship between kin and kindness. It is finding a relationship between loneliness and violence. It is discovering the human capacity for massive violence toward itself, its kind, and others. Is this behavior giving distance to humans and apes? Fowler writes:

> is this really an ape? i thought you were forever
> to make free with your pike
> a cock joke this early, rolled the dinosaur?
> what the bloody hell is this massive weapon?
> splits us homidae from the pan pongo interface[5]

Here the familiar roles are reversed, and the dinosaur represents the old distance calling out the arrogance of humanity. The older siblings have been scandalized by the behavior of the youngest. Here the pike and the massive weapon might also be a euphemism for a penis standing erect as humans stand. To be young is often to be rude in the sense of full health and sexuality. It is discovering forever is not a thing realized in a lifetime. Humans are only a part of the whole ape family, Hominidae, a party to aging and evolution. Fowler is locating humans between the faces of the pongo genus orangutans and the pan genus chimpanzee and bonobo. The gorilla is alone left out of the conversation, an unfortunate fate. Here is the ambiguity of family interactions, at once.

Family life unrolls the individual in the world. The development of an individual recapitulates the evolution of language in the overly verbal apes.

---

5. ibid., p.101.

The first person singular is capitalized, indeed; it is the only pronoun that is capitalized when used in the middle of sentence as well as the beginning. This is a kind of domestication of the poem moving it toward standard punctuation. Fowler writes:

> *I am here*
> and out of the hospital
> of origins
> comes I
> *I*
> one slant line down
> which skeletons language forever
> poetry
> and entirely everything else also⁶

Is the first person singular endlessly selfish in its self-reference. The skeleton itself recalls the first person singular in that it is mostly long thin bones slightly curved. Is the first person singular endlessly selfish in its self-reference. To skeleton is to kill with starvation. It is only illustrating and telling to include birth and remains in the human narrative. The first person is singular and alone. The first person singular is a profile for humans standing tall. Can the language of the overly verbal apes be reduced to self-reflection to interacting with ourselves?

The first person had to unfold. The unfolding of the first person recapitulates the unrolling of language. Evolution and development must interact. Fowler illustrates this series of events. When he capitalizes the first person in the human poem, it is a rare case of following convention. Here the first person is now towering over the lower case letters; it is overwhelming other ways of making sense of the way language falls on the page. It is only too human to find meaning must be endlessly self-referential. Poet Iris Colomb considers making meaning while improvising with musicians at SKRONK's open sessions between July 2021 and August 2022. In her essay, *Improvising with text: things to unlearn*, she writes:

> Sound makes me wary of the weight of language, that consuming propensity to point, define and explain. Here, language is one of many sounds, it must not overpower. I try to use meaning with caution. I avoid the 'I', favor connective words, pick out ubiquitous phrases, weave speech into patterns, let them contract, expand and collapse.⁷

---

6. ibid., pp.101-102.

7. Colomb, Iris, "Text as Instrument: Improvising with Musicians', English Studies in Latin America, Issue 24, <https://letras.uc.cl/wp-content/uploads/2023/01/FULL-issue24.pdf> [accessed 2 January 2023] pp. 69-77.

It is interactions all the way down the sound. The roll language plays here is very much becoming a part of the whole landscape. Colomb is concerned that the first person is an invasive species which will remove complexity by overwhelming the environment. The first person singular is a profile for humans overshadowing the great apes.

The first person is a metaphor for how humans understand and misunderstand evolutionary biology. It is a failure of appreciation as seen in the various forms interacting. In the *Plant Time Manifold Transcripts*, JH Prynne parodies the equation of vertical height with evolutionary superiority. He writes:

> The metaphor of relative elevation in the hierarchy of morphogenetic sophistication is all too crudely suggestive. And though of course I respect your own scr-r-ruptulous objectivity there are too many today who confuse height above ground with innate developmental superiority.

Here is the very awareness that the first person singular is in fact self-elevating at the expense of others present. He mocks the self-congratulatory carrot in conflict with the drunken lichen. It is easy to laugh at a talking carrot. It is far too removed from human sympathies and therefore fails to alter them. Self-reflection is essential to learning. Fowler understands that it is the very human vanity that facilitates learning. The human poem is meant to be a leaning experience.

Let us unroll the ways in which Fowler was influenced by Prynne. It is an opportunity to follow the unrolling of experimental British poetry and the unfolding of a particular poet in parallel. In his 2015 interview with Will Barrett for Sabotage Reviews, he effusive with his praise for Prynne. Fowler writes:

> His poetry is a lifetime engagement for the reader with the possibilities of language and meaning. It is inspiring, at times breathtaking. Moreover, what I take to be his gentle resistance to having his biographical details overwhelm the actual content of his poetry ... is admirable.[8]

Fowler and Prynne are united by a willingness allow language to overshadow their lives. In their writing they foreground language and background themselves in order to more fully explore the power for language to reflect itself back to itself. Language as a lens for looking back at itself. It is the

---

8. Will Barrett, '"It's all one enormous blancmange" – an interview with S J Fowler', *Sabotage Reviews*, 10th March 2015 <http://sabotagereviews.com/2015/03/10/its-all-one-enormous-blancmange-an-interview-with-s-j-fowler/> [accessed 25th August 2022].

power of language to overwhelm the human mind that these poets want to explore. Here is humanity found in the background of its own mind's eye. Let us take this as confirmation that Prynne has had some influence on the ways in which Fowler's poetry has unfolded.

Self-reflection is an entanglement of image and language. How humans see determines how they see themselves and how they make that image into language. There might be natural limits to self-reflection. Fowler is inquiring into the relationship between literature and photography as reflective surfaces. He writes:

> how like humans to blur its photography
> how like humans to be on instagram while writing
> how like humans to have stereoscopic vision
> grasping hands the abolity to climb[9]

He is showing how image and language interact in different contexts. He is showing how minor alterations in the spelling of a word can blur its meaning along with its image. It is not a question of errors. Rather it is an inquiry into the way the human mind makes sense. It is exploring spelling. Here is exploring meaning making in a mind bending way. It is testing itself to figure out how effectively language can reflect the meaning inside a human mind.

Fowler has followed the evolution of literature so far his inquiry has turned into the evolution of language and the human mind. The human poem becomes an inquiry into the relationship between mind and eyesight. Naturally, it is observing language in hindsight. It is simultaneously using language to describe vision. In the Encyclopedia of Neuroscience, AJ Parker notes that 'in current usage, stereoscopic vision often refers uniquely to the sense of depth derived from the two eyes'.[10] A sense of depth is essential for grasping and climbing. It is juxtaposed to the two dimensional nature of Instagram and in general, the superficiality of social media. Here is really a metaphor for three-dimensional thinking. It is the interplay of image and language layered over over again to give a nuanced understanding of the human mind.

The figure matters. The language that we use to turn ourselves into figures matters. It is not enough for Fowler to have a metaphor work as a bridge between the known and unknown. He is interested in the ways language accumulates. It is the ways in which language is turned into literature, is layered, and falls all over itself finally. He writes:

---

9. SJ Fowler, *The Great Apes*, p.105.
10. AJ Parker, 'Stereoscopic Vision', in *Encyclopedia of Neuroscience*, ed. by Larry R. Squire (Cambridge, Massachusetts: Academic Press, 2009) p. 411.

> to chronesthesia
> to autonesis
> how like humans to be so gold
> how like humans to mental time travel
> how like humans to pretend it cares[11]

Anaphora at once means carry back in place or time. Fowler leans into this definition by beginning a five page anaphora with three references to time travel. Here is a reminder to the reader that humanity is the youngest oldest member of the hominid family, and so how it knows itself is mostly through memory. The human mind will always need to turn back to be returning to earlier times in order to make meaning. It is even the nature of figurative language.

Anaphora figures a mountain of humanity. The repetition is simply illustrating the accumulation of humanity. It is the repeated references to humanity as a monolithic whole that gives the poem a distant tone. So much proximity is magnifying the pores and the blemishes. It is intimacy and distain. For cognitive scientist Douglas Hoftstadter writes that 'deep understanding of causality sometimes requires the understanding of very large patterns and their abstract relationships and interactions, not just the understanding of microscopic objects interacting in microscopic time intervals'.[12] Here is the matter of perspective or the perspective of what is the matter with humanity. Where each line begins with the universal human and ends with something specific to humanity, there is disdain next to distinction. It is an inquiry into the dark side of self-reflection, when it looks more like a funhouse mirror. Human nature distances itself from itself.

There is a fine line between fun and disgust. It is fun for one person to boast, but disgusting for another to listen to the boasting. To boast is overrate to romanticize to make into armor. Here is revealed a deep human need to adorn themselves to their achievements. It is a way to armor themselves. Fowler writes:

> how like humans to love and admit it
> how like humans to have a distinctive upper surface
> amassed with boats[13]

Admit also known as allow to enter to tolerate to listen to be compatible with love. Here is a boast floating on an oceanic feeling of love. This is a criticism

---

11. SJ Fowler, *The Great Apes*, p.103.
12. Douglas Hofstadter, *I Am A Strange Loop*, (New York, New York: Basic Books, 2008) p.41.
13. SJ Fowler, *The Great Apes*, p.107.

of romantic love being elevated beyond the monstrosity of human need. It is an inquiry into the confessional line as a kind falsity, a false dichotomy, and symmetry only means a funhouse mirror taken as serious reality.

It is no more a funhouse mirror. Here is a plan of symmetry to understand the way the body unfolds. It is the anterior-posterior axis which is a line of symmetry falling from the mouth to the colloquial tail. A fine line is falling between love and sexual intercourse. Fowler writes:

> how like humans to have a distinctive lower mudded
> surface full of treasure
> how like humans to hate and enjoy it
> how like humans to scorch, yellow or darken its waves and
> wilt[14]

Sex is a reflection. It is not a question of good or bad intentions. It is a question of how self-reflection can compound and double human intentions. The human poem is taking sex as synecdoche; a part telling how we interact with similar beings, how we behave as a part of the world. It makes the ways in which humanity mistreats the planet into the body of the problem here. Where the yellow waves are damaged hair. There are the literally polluted waters and the metaphorical call of the pale horse of the apocalypse. Let us follow this perversity from under the microscope to the farthest range of the telescope; this is the nature of the human poem.

Let us love the perverse. Humans love to hate the planet and we hate to love the planet. Humanity will continue to pervert it until it drowns us, burns us, chokes us, and becomes little more than a mirror of horrors. Fowler writes:

> and the erectus articulates oh yeah
> the hand of earth demonstrates the law of equilibrium
> is the foremost law of the universe[15]

The erectus refers to humanity. The erectus reads aloud as a homophonic translation for erect us. The hand of earth stands for the hand working the erection toward release, because it is a stress release mechanism. The law of chemical equilibrium states that when stress is applied to a system in thermodynamic equilibrium, then the system will move equilibrium in the direction that reduces the stress. 'Oh yeah' is a simple affirmation or a recollection of half-forgotten information that is important to solving a problem. The hand is standing for the role of climate change in fucking

---

14. ibid., p.107.
15. ibid., p.107

human life. We love to hate sex and we hate to love sex. Yet humanity cannot outrun the consequences of our interactions, because the universe is the fourth person singular.

The fourth person singular is not a person, not only a person; it is everything in the universe. It is an act of humility to acknowledge the fourth person singular. Fowler wants to own the knowledge that humanity can never get outside its interactions with the fourth person singular. Karen Barad writes:

> Knowing is not an ideational affair, or a capacity that is the exclusive birthright of the human. Knowing is a material practice, a specific engagement of the world where part of the world becomes differentially intelligible to another part of the world in its differential accountability to or for that of which it is a part.[16]

Sex is differentially intelligible; it is a relationship between the part and whole. It is a kind of accountability inside and outside the body. It is the play of exploration and excitement coming together in one tense moment interaction giving over to the accumulation of knowledge. Orgasm might be the moment of measurement for the scientist. The best experiments will only be meaningful if they are interpreted in a way that will help us understand our place within the universe.

Let us consider listening. Let us explore sexual intercourse as listening to another person. It is interchange, it is changing the space between two similar beings, it is stretching oneself further into another. It is turning into a question of giving and receiving. The human poem moves from the very far distant past into the near future. Here is a human narrative turning from the breadth of evolutionary history to the depths of the mind making sense of itself. The human poem zooms in and out of focus. The human poem moves between a microscope and telescope. It literally fails to focus in favor of shifting rapidly between interpretive lens best suited to discuss the following associations. It is metonymic kind of organization. It is following its own tail and it is following the ways in which tacit knowledge is made explicit. It is following the relationship between the cognitive unconscious and the storyteller in the form of a poem. Fowler writes:

> favored by nature? fortune refuses
> fortune showers? nature maltreats[17]

---

16. Karen Barad, *Meeting the Universe Halfway* (Durham, North Carolina: Duke University Press, 2007) p.280.

17. SJ Fowler, *The Great Apes*, p.107.

Fortune and nature are the third person singular. If fortune is father and inheritance, then nature is the abbreviation for mother nature. If and only if life itself a screen, then it gives a diffraction pattern. The first person is not enough. The first person must turn into the listener for the second person. The limit of knowledge is the limit of the human ability to listen and mirror what it hears inside other minds.

Let us experiment inside fruit flies. The fruit fly has a sense of place inside and outside the body. Cells listen to other cells in the unfolding in order to find out how they will figure in the body. Cells in the fly body developing learn their positional values. Developmental biologist Lewis Wolpert writes:

> the positional values in the leg and antenna of the fly are the same. Both are quite long structures, projecting one from the body, the other from the head, but with very different shapes. However, a mutation in a single gene can result in the fly developing a leg instead of an antenna projecting from the head.[18]

It is important to note regular legs will develop. It is only a simple mutation that leads to legs unfolding on the head instead. There is an either / or relationship between the antennae and legs in fruit fly genetics that give the head to tail pattern. Cells listen to learn the instructions given by the Antennapedia gene. Cells like humans learn by interaction.

The human poem is a love affair with listening to similar beings, our siblings in order to better learn to our needs. The first person singular is forever a grey sieve. The second person singular is sifting through the cell cultures and looking outwards. The third person singular is shifting focus between the foreign and familiar of the similar beings. Drosophila also known as fruit fly means lover of dew. Fowler uses a microscopic and a telescopic lens for understanding the place of humanity in the world. It is important to note the positional learning all the way down. Evolutionary biology is the telescopic lens because it makes a single human life insignificant by means of the enormous breadth of space and time. Evolutionary biology is the telescopic lens because it locates humanity within all space and time. The length of evolutionary time is juxtaposed to the brevity of the human life time also known as developmental time. It all falls inside the fourth person singular also known as the universe. The third and fourth person can be heard.

Drosophila is the third person singular. In the sense that the fruit fly is representative of life foreign and familiar on the planet. It is different enough to humanity that only a simple mutation will lead to antennae unfolding instead of legs for the body of the problem. If legs give strength,

---

18. Lewis Wolpert, *How We Live and Why we Die: The Secret Lives of Cells* (London: Faber, 2009) p.97.

then antennae get to take strength by means of listening to the outside world. Legs cannot be meek, only be weak, but antennae can be meek. Indeed, one cannot be meek without listening and the hearing organ resides in the antennae in fruit flies. If humans choose to identify with the function of their legs defying gravity and dividing them from the great apes, then they cannot be meek. In a world dominated by overly verbal apes, it is listening not speaking that makes one meek. It is making oneself meek before the planet. Here is the answer to the question that concludes the human poem. Humans can be meek if and only if they choose to soften their footprints and identify with the function of their ears. Let us imagine ears in the place of the unrolling of further bipedal evil. To be mild before the wildlife. To be wild before the monstrosity of human needs and destruction. To be mindful enough for the full unfolding and unrolling of life found in the fourth person singular also known as the universe.

Works Cited:

Barad, Karen, *Meeting the Universe Halfway* (Durham, North Carolina: Duke University Press, 2007)

Barrett, Will, '"It's all one enormous blancmange" – an interview with S J Fowler', *Sabotage Reviews*, 10th March 2015 <http://sabotagereviews.com/2015/03/10/its-all-one-enormous-blancmange-an-interview-with-s-j-fowler/> [accessed 25th August 2022]

Colomb, Iris, "Text as Instrument: Improvising with Musicians', English Studies in Latin America, Issue 24, <https://letras.uc.cl/wp-content/uploads/2023/01/FULL-issue24.pdf> [accessed 2nd January 2023] pp. 69-77.

Dalke, Anne and Grobstein, Paul, 'Three-Dimensional Story Telling: An Exploration of Teaching Reading, Writing, and Beyond', *Journal of Teaching Writing*. 2007 <https://serendipstudio.org/~pgrobste/pdfs/3DStoryTelling07.pdf> [accessed 10th August 2022]

Fowler, SJ, *The Great Apes*, (Rhydwen, Wales: Broken Sleep Books, 2022)

Hofstadter, Douglas, *I Am A Strange Loop*, (New York, New York: Basic Books, 2008)

Parker, AJ, 'Stereoscopic Vision', in *Encyclopedia of Neuroscience*, ed. by Larry R. Squire (Cambridge, Massachusetts: Academic Press, 2009)

Wolpert, Lewis, *How We Live and Why we Die: The Secret Lives of Cells* (London: Faber, 2009)

Unfoldingorilla

Evolution and development are intertwined. The gorilla poem is the second of five poems in SJ Fowler's collection, *The Great Apes*, published by Broken Sleep Books. Fowler and Kent have utilized the layout to create a mirror here. The gorilla is seeing the chimpanzee facing page as an imperfect reflection or refraction of himself. He must reconcile himself to this comparison. Here is gorilla as the adolescent sibling, older, and acutely full of new powers. Fowler is exploring the ways in which irony and self-reflection are intertwined in adolescent development – adolescence being the stage in which self-awareness begins and the individual expands and pushes on everything in an attempt to define self.

    Adolescence is also an inquiry into the evolution and development of monsters. It is unrolling. It is the gorilla discovering his own powers. He is measuring his powers in order to find where he will fit into the hierarchy. Here is the myth of adolescence; the role of Herakles labors is to test his powers against those society names monsters. Carson has unfolded the Herakles character in order to show the unrolling narrative of the relationship between heroes and monsters. What undoes Herakles is falling in love with a monster. Carson portrays Geryon as older less powerful or more passive with each retelling of the myth. Love like violence has the power to overwhelm. In her fourth retelling of the myth, *H of H Playbook* shows it is only a thread as threshold dividing heroes and monsters.[1] It might be that monsters are simply older heroes.

    Adolescence is twisting between feeling too old and too young simultaneously. It unfolds as a hyperawareness of foolishness. The gorilla finds himself curious about the consequences, intentions, and the tension between them. Fowler is intertwining normal adolescent development with evolutionary biology by giving the gorilla his own observations about humanity. He writes:

---

1. Anne Carson, *H of H Playbook* (London, UK: Jonathan Cape 2021).

> why do you think
> people are this why?[2]

Here the replacement of 'way' with 'why' shows the gorilla is interested in hypocrisy. The origin of hypocrisy is feigning. To pretend to determine to judge and act a part on the stage of life. It is intentional falsity. Hypocrisy is the dissimulation of real character in order to hide beliefs; it might be a fear response; it might be a response to society.

Adolescence is learning to revise and retell stories. Fowler is mining the gorillas as a metaphor for the adolescent human mind. The gorilla is a void, avoiding violence, the gorilla is afraid and the smell of fear has been observed by humans, the role of a silverback is to lead the family away from violence to help the family avoid violence. To be aggressive in displaying in order to avoid violence. A grey sieve is a silverback gorilla. A sign the leader has the lived experience to tell when to fight. It is important to note that interactions between gorillas, even between family units, need not result in violence. Gorillas, like countries, can communicate and be diplomatic. Here is an inquiry into unfolding violent tendencies as a great ape develops, into the nature of violence and the violence of nature.

Herakles is the perfect adolescent here, because he is halfway between god and human. His labors unfold his powers inside him. The gods are children drunk on power with no fear of death and the humans are mortal, so always obsessed with the consequences of their actions and potential loss. The gorilla relates to humans in the same way that humans relate to gods. It is alienation all the way down adolescence. Fowler writes:

> you ain't
> just you in the world you smell like a time of ratchets
> and not the one we miss with beedays[3]

This is a visceral disgust for humanity with its bidets and birthdays. The gorilla does not see us as siblings. Humans might be similar beings with magic or more advanced technologically. Then there we have gods are fearless children running around with their eyes glued down to iPhones for the gorilla. The gorilla is flirting with evil and foreshadowing the human poem.

The gorilla is questioning whether evil and evolution are twin natures in this world. Evil unrolling like a ball down a hill. It is silence in the face of evil, violence, and evolution are bound in christian theology. Here is where the gorilla overlaps with de Sade. Fowler overleaps de Sade with Darwin and with his sexual selection theory and the possibilities it opens. The fibers of the narrative fall into a philosophy that leave the gorilla feeling he will be

---

2. SJ Fowler, *The Great Apes*, (Rhydwen, Wales: Broken Sleep Books, 2022) p.50.
3. SJ Fowler, *The Great Apes*, p.43.

unevolved because he is not violent and unloved because he is unevolved. This is an exploration of the unfolding violence and unrolling sexuality in human society. It is an inquiry into the evolution of stories and the stories of evolution.

Stories unfold over individual lifetimes. The gorilla experiments with folding himself away with rolling up the threads of the narrative and taking his ball home. Here is the heart as soft feeling and the hard minded as its inverse; inside the human being. There is always movement backward and forward like drumsticks. Fowler writes:

> are for his heart three or four times less sensitive
> are for three or four times as much power of reason
> are for what you call hard-heartedness[4]

He is following the percussive moments inside. Thinking to thickening. Here is the human admiring the size of the gorilla cardiac muscle. The human needs to understand the walls will show power and wisdom coming from the silverback. Thickening to thinking the gorilla has grown old in human years.

Here we turn to see the life history of a hero unfolding Herakles. This reverses the sex and violence metaphor. Here are bodies booming into their powers physical and intellectual, it is an illustration neuroanatomy in the ears and the mind. There is a sensitivity to humans even inside a life history of violence. Coalflowers are cauliflowers. Cauliflower comes from the name for adolescent plants in the cole family. This is serious play with homophones and hearing. Carson writes:

> It popped his ear you
> see melted coalflowers run out his ear.
> they are black and hot. They aren't real[5]

A cauliflower ear is distorted by blows of a fellow fighter or the weather-like wishes of gods. Iris and Lyssa blossom madness in the mind of Herakles. The gods disfigure Herakles through his ears, his brain, and his labors, and his story of violence is inseparable from a history of violence. The coal inside is the combustible accumulation of loss and impulse and leads to the loss of impulse control. It is black and hot blood dark after a time inside dried. Madness and trauma might mean chronic traumatic encephalopathy formerly dementia pugilistica.

Coalflowers are a metaphor for a life history of violence. Here the ears are telling. It is listening to the gods that makes Herakles ears bloom. When gods speak to humans it is heard a blow delivered the head to turn around

---

4. SJ Fowler, *The Great Apes*, p.48.

5. Anne Carson, *H of H Playbook* (London, UK: Jonathan Cape 2021)

to the different future. Carson is measuring the gods power by showing the ways in which they impact humanity. She writes:

> coalflowers that's just the name we
> give to popped brain crystals when they
> run out your ear you have no more
> sense of how the world is level if lights[6]

It is a black concussion. Here is the brain bruised and disoriented inside the human body. The result is a loss of balance or the sense of balance or the sense of proprioception which balances our bodies with the rest of the world. Brain crystals are identity stories that have crystallized inside the mind.

It is stories not turtles all the way down human minds. It is the asymmetry here the enemy of the human is the human mind damning the gorilla also. There is inquiry into storytelling and retelling. The gorilla and human minds are retellings of the primate mind that can sit beside each other. There is a preposition for this positioning feeling. In *Touching Feeling*, Eve Kosofsky Sedgwick explores the meaning of the word beside. She writes:

> *Beside* is an interesting preposition also because there is nothing very dualistic about it; a number of elements may lie alongside one another, though not an infinity of them. Its interest does not, however, depend on a fantasy of metonymically egalitarian or even pacific relations, as any child knows who's shared a bed with siblings. *Beside* comprises a wide range of desiring, identifying, representing, repelling, paralleling, differentiating, rivaling, learning, twisting, mimicking, withdrawing, attracting, aggressing, warping, and other relations.[7]

How a story does sit beside its own retelling is not unlike how a human might sit beside a gorilla or how a monster might sit beside a human. Here is a collection of literary kinds inside the stories of evolution and the evolution of stories.

There is a sense in which the gorilla is anxious about the ways he will unfold into maturity beside himself and humanity and the environment. The gorilla is like the tween, teen, twenty-something human being in its understanding of the world. It is finding evil everywhere near and far and yet ambivalent. Fowler writes:

---

6. Ibid.
7. Kosofsky Sedgwick, Eve, *Touching Feeling: Affect, Pedagogy, Performativity* (Durham: North Carolina: Duke University Press, 2003 p.8.

> with his I don't know what anxiety is
> with his you fill the bowls shape and in the past you would
> be fine[8]

The gorilla wants us to know that the future is uncertain. This is not to be overstated from a species that has been very endangered due to human activity. It is the knowing tone of someone young who has seen more than his generation. It possible to think of the great apes as representations of the life history of human beings. Each chapter uses an ape to focus on an aspect of human development. The gorilla is late adolescence, knowing a little too much to be comfortable with himself or his peers.

The gorilla is discovering his mind unfolding. There is a keen sense of literary kinship in retelling a story to reach into the new ecosystem inside the adolescent mind. The ways in which we interpret literature can find kin and kindness. Fowler retells Lesson 11 from the Tao Te Ching in a single line inside a long section of anaphora in the gorilla. He selects the word bowl to echo hole and whole and clay pot. Here is adolescence described. The Tao Te Ching says:

> We join spokes together in a wheel,
> But it is the center hole
> That makes the wagon move.
>
> We shape clay into a pot,
> But it is the emptiness inside
> That holds whatever we want.[9]

It is important to note the distinction between filling and fulfilling. The gorilla poem is making the point that capitalism makes for filling without becoming full. The gorilla knows he holds the potential for unfolding a different humankind through the evolution of literature and the literature of evolution.

Knowledge unrolls and unfolds in literature. Carson and Fowler both obsess over the possibility that literature can move a monster. Carson is interested in how a hero unrolls into a monster. Fowler is interested in how what was once seen as a perfect creature can unfold itself into corruption. Here is a metaphor for what the adolescent seeks in society. There is the black back gorilla looking for a family to fit into the ecosystem meaning the future. Then there is what is monstrous and cannot fit into the environment

---

8. SJ Fowler, *The Great Apes*, p.42.
9. 'Lesson 11', *Tao Te Ching*, trans. Stephen Mitchell (New York City, New York: Harper & Row Books, 1988).

ever, which is where Herakles finds himself and moves to save himself in the ending of the *H of H Playbook*. Neither the gods nor the gorilla will save humanity from its corruption. It is only humanity that might save itself from itself if it can look past its own perceived perfection in the worlds of Carson and Fowler. They inquire if moving forward is ever anything more than atavism; is progress always waiting behind; is lamenting gorilla and orangutan the human future?

Let us tell a story about the future of the adolescent and his relationship with adulthood in Carson and Fowler's writing. The story of the future is held inside self-reflection is turning around revising the story is turning around the evolution of literature is turning around the development of the writer. In *Dancing at the Edge of the World*, Ursula K LeGuin, writes in the chapter titled 'Science Fiction and the Future':

> The future lies behind – behind your back, over your shoulder. The future is what you can't see, unless you turn around and kind of snatch a glimpse. And then sometimes you wish you hadn't, because you've glimpsed what is sneaking up on you from behind ...[10]

To look back to catch the future and to return to facing forward to facing oneself in the mirror in practice. The chimp is still found in the mirror and the bonobo is behind. The movement of the gorilla poem is fouettés to whip to be whipping powerful turns around returns to encircle oneself completely for a moment. The nature of adolescence is to be whipping oneself inwards.

Hypocrisy is a way of saying that there is an internal story and an external story. Herakles labors were acts of violence. His labors were an internal and external story until he fell in love with the monster Geryon, and then, the labors were only an external story. *H of H Playbook* is the narrative of what happened once Herakles became a hypocrite. According to the *Oxford English Dictionary*, hypocrisy is 'assuming of a false appearance of virtue or goodness, with dissimulation of real character or inclinations, esp. in respect of religious life or beliefs; hence in general sense, dissimulation, pretence, sham'.[11] Here is holding stories about oneself and ones role in human society that might be alternate, compatible, or perfectly hypocritical. It is storytelling all the way down to a story about two stories. Carson and Fowler are obsessed with adolescence because they are obsessed with hypocrisy and adolescence is the age that discovers hypocrisy.

The gorilla is obsessed with the hypocrisy of human nature. Fowler is inquiring if human excitement might ever be more than the intertwining

---

10. LeGuin, Ursula K, *Dancing at the Edge of the World* (New York City, New York: Grove Press, 1989) p.142.

11. Editors of the Oxford English Dictionary, 'Hypocrisy', *Oxford English Dictionary* (Oxford, UK: Oxford University Press, 2023).

of violence and admiration. He is utilizing sex as a metaphor for violence. He is unrolling the story that humans have an evolved relationship with violence. It is dissimulation all the way down an earlier gorilla poem titled, 'Bodily Absence'. He writes:

> They say the gorilla
> had the child to protect it.
> I don't think so.
> It's some kind of magical resonance from then,
> the past,
> my poem about horrible violence,
> that so many timeless idiots
> find more offensive
> than the actual violence[12]

Here the child appears as evidence of past sexual excitement that is paired with past violence in the poem. 'Bodily Absence' was published in *The Guide to Being Bear Aware*, which is Fowler's second book of satirical anthropomorphism; so it is a similar book or sibling to *The Great Apes*. It shows the unfolding relationship between poetry and violence in his writing.

Fowler reflects on 'Bodily Absence' in the gorilla poem. Here he is writing with a great distance to illustrate the distain one great ape feels for another's needs being hidden in hypocrisy. It is the innocence of the gorilla and his simple irony that reveal what humans conceal. He writes:

> are they all celibates?
> if so, the animal is damned
> to extinction
> a funny little laugh in gorilla's sleep
> if not, what a fine line
> to be so unbodily
> and then need it from time to time[13]

The human damned is the gorilla doomed. What a fine line refers to first person, the state of being erect which itself could refer to sexual excitement or man standing on two legs, or simply a poem. Here is an inquiry into the nature of the body, sexual intercourse, and coexisting on this planet. There is so much failure to face in the violence between human interactions, gorilla interactions, and human-gorilla interactions.

The *H of H Playbook* is unfolding the relationship between humans and similar beings. It is spinning an inquiry into reversals. Herakles fell in love

---

12. Fowler, SJ, *The Guide to Being Bear Aware* (Bristol, UK: Shearsman, 2018) p.12
13. SJ Fowler, *The Great Apes*, p.53.

with a monster, killed the monster, and found the monstrous inside himself. His story unrolls a history of violence. Casey Cep writes:

> Carson is writing not only about the persistence of violence but about the possibility of redemption, and in this respect 'H of H' isn't just a playbook for the past. It is also, in the other sense of the word, a playbook for the future.[14]

In order to look into the future, one must turn around, because the future is behind us. Carson and Fowler have identified the persistence of violence as a blindspot in human society; it will be our future even if we refuse to turn around and look. They are both obsessed with teaching humans how to look at their monstrous selves in the mirror.

Humanity feigns to have put violence into the past, and yet, there is violence behind humanity, which is to say that there is violence in the future. Fowler utilizes the gorilla for adolescence and a hyper sensitivity to hypocrisy in order to unfold his satirical anthropomorphism.[15] It is important to return to the adolescent as the foundation for self-reflection. It is sensitivity to hypocrisy that will save humanity by means of telling the story of humanity and retelling it until it is less harmful for everyone. Carson and Fowler are both obsessed with the telling and retelling of the story of human beings as a story. Theirs is an inquiry into hypocrisy into unrolling the stories inside hypocritical behavior in order to better understand humanity. We can learn from the ways in which their inquiries continue to unfold. Here is an inquiry into the role humanity plays in unfolding the evolution of literature and the literature of evolution.

---

14. Cep, Casey, 'Anne Carson's Obsession with Herakles', *The New Yorker Books*, The New Yorker, 8th Nov 2021 <https://www.newyorker.com/magazine/books/11/08/anne-carsons-obsession-with-herakles> [accessed 10 December 2022].

15. Fowler, SJ, A 'note on : The Great Apes published in April with Broken Sleep Books' *SJ Fowler Blog*, 25 Jan 2022, <https://steven-fowler-1pys.squarespace.com/blog?offset=1643839867400> [accessed 10 February 2023].

Works Cited

Carson, Anne, *H of H Playbook* (London, UK: Jonathan Cape 2021)

Cep, Casey, 'Anne Carson's Obsession with Herakles', *The New Yorker Books*, The New Yorker, 8 Nov 2021 <https://www.newyorker.com/magazine/books/11/08/anne-carsons-obsession-with-herakles> [accessed 10th December 2022]

Editors of the Oxford English Dictionary, 'Hypocrisy', *Oxford English Dictionary* (Oxford, UK: Oxford University Press, 2023)

Fowler, SJ, *The Guide to Being Bear Aware* (Bristol, UK: Shearsman, 2018)

Fowler, SJ, *The Great Apes*, (Rhydwen, Wales: Broken Sleep Books, 2022)

Fowler, SJ, A 'note on : The Great Apes published in April with Broken Sleep Books' *SJ Fowler Blog*, 25th Jan 2022, <https://steven-fowler-1pys.squarespace.com/blog?offset=1643839867400> [accessed 10th February 2023]

Kosofsky Sedgwick, Eve, *Touching Feeling: Affect, Pedagogy, Performativity* (Durham: North Carolina: Duke University Press, 2003)

LeGuin, Ursula K, *Dancing at the Edge of the World* (New York City, New York: Grove Press, 1989)

'Lesson 11', *Tao Te Ching*, trans. Stephen Mitchell (New York City, New York: Harper & Row Books, 1988)

A Palimpsest Ape

Written on the body is a secret code only visible in certain lights; the accumulations of a lifetime gather there. In places the palimpsest is so heavily worked that the letters feel like braille. I like to keep my body rolled up away from prying eyes. Never unfold too much, tell the whole story. I didn't know that Louise would have reading hands. She has translated me into her own book.[1]

The bonobo poem is an open ended inquiry into the nature of history and the history of nature. It is important to note that humans write history; therefore, it reflects human nature and the ways in which humanity sees itself fitting into nature. Here is where satirical anthropomorphism illustrates the limits of human imagination. The bonobo poem is a consideration of the nature of the great great great grandfather ape, where he is the metaphorical last common ancestor for bonobos and humans. Here is a turn from the enumeration of human sins in the gorilla poem toward curiosity. There is a nuanced discussion of what behaviors might be atavistic and what behaviors might be recidivist in humans and bonobos both.

The nature of history is selection unrolling. Where the selection is determined in history, descent with modification is the evolution of literature and the literature of evolution. Fowler wants to explore the ways in which the evolution of literature can influence the development of an individual writer. For him, imagination is constrained, it is contained by history, it is made with the existing literature through descent with modification. The bonobo poem is laying out Fowler's theory of imagination. Sex is a metaphor for imagination, sexual acts stand in the stead of evolutionary traits, and it is the selection in the enumerated list to move toward consent and kink and behavior traditionally associated with pornography and bonobos that is surprisingly neither atavistic or recidivist.

The literature of evolution is unrolling in the natural world. Fields unfold. If fields continue to unfold, they will be found growing into surprising interdisciplinary places. Evolutionary theory and pornography find themselves side by side biology. Fowler writes:

> bonobo is reading this and thinking I am tame
> compared to homosap ingenuity
> and bonobo is rereading this and getting erect[2]

---

1. Jeanette Winterson, *Written on the Body*, (New York City: Vintage, 1994) p. 20.
2. SJ Fowler, The Great Apes, p. 64.

The scientific name for humans, homo sapiens is same wise is abbreviated to turn the meaning into homosaps is same saps. Sap is also a part of the history of evolution that makes beautiful fools. In the obsolete and transitive sense it is more explicitly to remove sap from wood and thus gives us a lovely botanical metaphor to further queer human sexual mores. The homosaps acts as a foil or a fool for the bonobo and by extension the wonobo reading the pornography of evolution. It suggests a human orgasm or a same orgasm that is to say that human and bonobo orgasms are the same or similar or homologous is to appeal to evolutionary biology.

The history of nature unrolls. Here is a fulfilling symmetry between orgasm and organism that experiences it. There is a fearful similarity between bonobos and humans in the nature of what it means to be seen as obscene. Women have been found to find bonobo sexual activity exciting themselves. Meredith L Chivers, director of Queen's University's sexuality and gender lab has observed this phenomenon in her research.[3] Fowler likewise utilizes women, bonobos, and wonobos to explore sexuality. He writes:

> 5. teaching a wonobo mutual masturbation out of sync
> 6. having a wonobo kneel on shoulders while he wacks
> 7. being impotent with wonobo[4]

A wonobo is a willing partner for the bonobo. A wonobo is willing to fulfill a bonobo and is fulfilled by the bonobo regardless of gender or species. The bonobo in the poem is knowing in an intellectual and physical sense, the bonobo knows that women and bonobos will respond to his sexuality.

The history of nature unfolds. The human need to understand is balanced by the limits of anthropomorphism. The same is true for the bonobo need to be understood by human beings, so it is a mixture of imagination and revision that is required. Fowler writes:

> one can hardly imagine in what diversity
> an ape can develop their debaucheries
> all they need is a permissive partner in crimes who can set
>   down in detail all those things
> when the imagination ape is inflamed, however great is
>   variety[5]

This could be a reference to pioneering work of Jane Goodall, Dian Fossey,

---

3. Meredith L Chivers and others, 'Gender and sexual orientation differences in sexual response to sexual activities versus gender of actors in sexual films', Journal of personality and social psychology vol. 93,6 (2007): 1108-21, doi:10.1037/0022-3514.93.6.1108-
4. ibid., p. 70.
5. ibid., p. 62.

Birutė Galdikas in the field of primatology. It underlines the relationship between subject and writer, where the subject talks back; the bonobo is signaling appreciation for being seen in this way. To be observing the observer and making observations is reversing the intellectual hierarchy. The bonobo is subject and not only an object of observation inside the poem is a partnership in crime in desire to see and be seen in needing to make revisions in that scene.

The pornography of nature unfolds, as does the nature of pornography. The origin of pornography is obscenity in the written form in a manner intended to stimulate human erotic responses. The bonobo poem is rewriting the nature of the obscene. If sex is a metaphor for imagination, then there is the relationship between the subject and writer to consider. Here is the bonobo both the muse inflaming the poet's imagination and the mentor recommending research to open the poet's imagination to more than is known. To what extent is research pornography and pornography research?

Pornography unrolls human nature. It is revealing the nature of a need to imagine to make images to find wilderness. The bonobo is asking if the need for the obscene as seen in pornographic images is limited to some humans or is species wide. Is it a falling back into sin as someone reoffending where pornography is the offense? Or is it simply humans behaving in the same ways as their ancestors as their great great great grandfather's morality is problems made in present time? Fowler writes:

> it is 1677 and the marquis de sade is writing
> what you thinking
> because he an ape aristocrat shaved just right
> to get in history[6]

It might be atavism by way of proving evolution by illustrating how species have changed over time. In the middle, Fowler is giving the reader a literary atavism. Form is following function in the adaptationist paradigm of evolutionary biology. Fowler might be pointing out that the very patriarchal fantasies realized in De Sade and pornography have as much potential to be read as atavistic as the homosocial behaviors of bonobos.

History unfolds. The features of the great great great grandfather ape matter. Here is an inquiry into nature and recidivism where the relationship between habit and inhabitant and society matters. Recidivism means a relapsing into crime, reoffending, a tendency to behave in the ways descried.[7] It is behavior that will unfold over the individual lifespan as a pattern. It is obvious that De Sade was a recidivist, it was his intention to sin and offend

---

6. ibid.,, p. 64.
7. 'Recidivism', *Oxford English Dictionary,* Oxford University Press < https://www.oed.com/dictionary/recidivism_n?tab=meaning_and_use#26568127> [accessed 1st June 2023]

and yet, he is still held more evolved than the bonobo. The hierarchical nature of religion and evolution is presented here. Fowler writes:

> a mistake apes are
> kin to make
> did Bonobo choose its will
> to urge?
> you think so don't you
> and makes Bonobo final pervato
> 74. love with righteous in the darkest sin[8]

Where rhyming kin and sin gives this satire, its satisfaction that the history of evolution is hypocritical. Kinship is often a question of kinds and kindnesses to similar beings even siblings in the unrolling sense that is only the history of evolution. Here is a reversal of the unrolling for the human to make kin with the bonobo. There would need to be a reversal, a receding of difference into history and recognition given to the bonobo impulse to make kin with humans. The notion that kin is made or manufactured in the sense of fact and fiction is hinting to philosophy of science.

Recidivism unfolds an individual history. It is ambiguous if the human or the bonobo is the recidivist here. The bonobo poem is an inquiry into the nature of the relationship between narrator and reader. Recalling the line: 'love with righteous in the darkest sin', here right echoes light and adds a visual element to the juxtaposition of sin and righteousness.[9] At the end of the numbered list echoing De Sade and recent scientific advances in understanding the great apes sexuality, is love. Love is a human construct, and yet, Fowler employs love at the end of a long list of human debauchery. Love with that which is right might mean to fall in love with that which is right as a sort of ends justify the means of sin or it might be pointing to hypocrisy to the act of pretending to be righteous even in sin. It is a question of sincerity and irony. Is sin like beauty in the eye of the beholder? In the gorilla poem, Fowler defines 'beauty as nothing other than the promise of happiness'.[10] In the bonobo, then sin is nothing other than the promise of happiness. This is to say this sin is beauty fulfilling its promise, beautifulfilling, it is a direct answer to the emptiness inside that begins the poem. What if that which is defined as sin by history is still fulfilling now that it is not always considered a sin.

Read the field. Here is where recidivism meets satirical anthropomorphism. Fowler is analyzing the ways in which primatologists have figured the

---
8. SJ Fowler, *The Great Apes*, p. 77.
9. ibid., p. 77.
10. ibid., p. 48.

bonobo as figurative language. He is offering literary criticism across the field of evolution. Let us turn inwards for a moment to reflect on the ways in which our writing, history, and figuring unfold. Lewis was a student in an interdisciplinary course where they unfolded and unrolled an inquiry into evolution and literature at Bryn Mawr College. Anne Dalke and Paul Grobstein co-taught the Stories of Evolution and Evolution of Stories course. It began as a writing intensive course for first year students offered spring 2004 and spring 2005; it was later offered as a middle level course cross-listed in the Biology and English Departments at Bryn Mawr College in the spring semesters of 2007, 2009, and 2011. Dalke and Grobstein write:

> We will experiment, in this course, with two interrelated and reciprocal inquiries: whether the biological concept of evolution is a useful one in understanding the phenomena of literature (in particular: the generation of new stories), and whether literature contributes to a deeper understanding of evolution.[11]

It is precisely this reciprocity that defines our reading of the great apes in general and the bonobo poem in particular. We see Fowler as reading and writing the story of primatology as story telling and story revision between individuals and different species. This is the story of the role of reading and writing two fields together.

History unfolds in the field. Recidivism is folding and unfolding the field over the individual lifetime. If failure to revise oneself lies at the core of recidivism, then it is gesturing toward the writing process, because writing is itself a kind of behavior. Then the concept of recidivism gives us insight into the folding and unfolding of literature. It is important to note that literature evolves over many lifetimes also by rewriting and by the contributions of many individuals. The field of literature is rolling and unrolling with history. Let us explore the role of the great great great grandfather ape in the literature of evolution and the evolution of literature.

The bonobo poem begins with the unrolling of all life. It takes the alphabet and atavism. It moves from chemistry and medieval life to the great great great grandfathers. Fowler writes:

> a
> con
> fus
> ion
> a chemical table of nightmare squires

---

11. Anne Dalke and Paul Grobstein, 'The Story of Evolution and the Evolution of Stories', *Serendip*, <https://serendipstudio.org/exchange/courses/evolit/s09> [accessed 15th September 2023]

whipping the sun
out of predictable slime[12]

A con is a confidence trick calling for a fuse, a slow burning heat, and fiction calls for an ion to give an electric charge recalling the trick comes a second time, then there is slime. It is orgasm and organism that is to say primordial all the way down now. Let us not leave out a nightmare, a mayor ruling overnight and his domain is a square and the squires that came before were whipping the sons in daylight. It is abusing the son, it is corporal punishment for him, and it is training the colt from the nightmare to be a warhorse. It is unrolling life itself and finding the death wish beside the great great great grandfather ape.

History is unfolding itself into a line of fathers standing in a field. Stephen Jay Gould is a grandfather ape interested in finding once and future grandfather apes. Here is an infinite regress where the history of evolution and evolution of history is a pair of mirrors reflecting one another. There is a frame, an image, and a set of limitations unfolding. Gould writes:

> Organisms, on the other hand, are directed and limited by their past. They must remain imperfect in their form and function, and to that extent unpredictable since they are not optimal machines. We can not know their future with certainty, if only because a myriad of quirky functional shifts lies within the capacity of any feature, however well adapted to a present role.[13]

It is great great great grandparent apes all the way down and upwards. It could be forward or backwards. It could be that we should read both ways to better understand the natural order. Satirical anthropomorphism might be understood as a reversal of the natural order, and therefore, reframed as a kind of intellectual atavism.

The role of our ancestors in unrolling life is surprising. In the original sense, it is returning, turning around itself, the fact of coming again to take action by means of turning back. In a legal sense, it is returning property or title or reversal of previous judgment. Let us look into atavism unrolling in language. Gould writes on Darwin writes on great great great grandfather traits unrolling:

> Darwin felt that atavisms held the key to many mysteries of variation, and he devoted an entire chapter to it, closing as I will with these words: The fertilized germ of one of the higher

---

12. SJ Fowler, *The Great Apes*, p. 61.
13. Stephen Jay Gould, *Hen's Teeth and Horse's Toes: Further Reflections in Natural History*, Reissue Edition, (New York City, New York: W.W.Norton & Company, 1994) p.65.

> animals ... is perhaps the most wonderful object in nature ... On the doctrine of reversion [atavism] ... the germ becomes a far more marvelous object, for, besides the ariable changes which it undergoes, we must believe that it is crowded with invisible characters ... separated by hundreds or even thousands of generations from the present time: and these characters, like those written on paper with invisible ink, lie ready to be evolved whenever the organization is disturbed by certain known or unknown conditions.[14]

The surprise unrolled inside us. The way life unrolled will always surprise and limit the imagination. It is not unlike a palimpsest. It is hinting toward that genetic code which is written inside the human and bonobo body beside literature.

Here is rewinding the field. The bonobo name reveals its history unrolling in many variations. The most striking of which is the wonobo signifying a willing sexual partner bonobo or a woman bonobo hybrid. Here is bonoobo, pronounced bo-new-bo to rhyme with poo and pooper in the section discussing anal sex. There is bonobbo, pronounced bo-nob-bo or bo-nob-oh for orgasm. Then the bonobo name itself has an uncertain origin; it might be borrowed from German; it might be borrowed from a language of the Congo river region. Fowler writes:

> bo's on time
> bon's not acceptable stereotypes
> bono's with your daughter she's fine having fun even
> bonob's hangs your head in ignomy
> bonobo's a circular artery[15]

It is also a purposeful reading from the shortest abbreviation only the first syllable to the full three syllable word. It might be meant to echo the bonobo, wonobo, and women? There is the anaphora listing and the numerical listing are complementary. Bo is a homonym for beau, or boyfriend is the beginning of the bonobo and the relationship. With the adding of letters and syllables this relationship plays out in a few lines as the bonobo grows into its identity, goes through phases, unfolds itself before the reader. The bonobo identity is circling back to the opening lines of the poem trying to define a pervert.

Rewilding or regarding wilding the field. Human beings have turned the bonobo into a pervert inside and outside. There is a second section

---

14. Stephen Jay Gould quoting Charles Darwin, *The Variation of Animals and Plants Under Domestication*, second edition, (London: John Murray, 1868)

15. SJ Fowler, *The Great Apes*, p. 63.

experimenting with the bonobo name at the end of the poem fulfilling the promise of the circular definition. Fowler writes:

> with bolobos
> and something that was not an evil then
> can surely not have become one since?
> a pretty boon is not allowed
> tempt bomoboi just because he made the mistake of
>   bringing it into this world[16]

Bolobo is a river town, a territory in the Democratic Republic of the Congo, and a potential origin of the bonobo name. The origin of evil is next to evolution recalling atavism and recidivism. Then a boon is an obsolete prayer or request. It is a gift, benefit, a thing that one had no claim to and yet was absent in the present sense. Here is the absent present in the bonobo name. Bomoboi might be read as bomb oh boy! a name that is summoning and warning simultaneously. It is warning about the bonobo or the future of the bonobo or the future of humanity in the nuclear world, where bomb always implies the worst of human ingenuity running its course.

  The building of bo, bon, bono, bonob to bonobo is itself a palimpsest for the evolution of literature and the literature of evolution. It is natural history being written down and hidden and hiding writing simultaneously. It is written on the bonobo and human bodies again. It is not merely a reflection of the ways in which the genome is changing inside; it is reveling the activity of the environment outside. The bonobo poem is always playing with source material, looking through the lens of history in order to recover a greater number of possibilities for the individual to unfold and unroll over a lifetime. The bonobo imagines it is both recidivistic behavior in the individual and atavistic in the human populations.

CODA:

The progeny of the great great great grandfather ape is born. This individual first traversed the entire ancestral path of each and every one of its forefathers while gestating in the womb. Birth represents a singularity in this history of possibilities with the manifestation of a new interpretation of all the genetic material passed on to a new and living history yet to be written. The newborn is a blank palimpsest. Its entire history is there, but hidden

---

16. ibid., p. 76.

behind invisible genetic code. Then the living individual begins to write on the blank page, creating the latest manuscript on this every changing palimpsest. The individual learns and grows over the course of its lifetime, gathering experience and finding ways to survive in its current environment. If it repeats or recedes to past behaviors commonly used from earlier periods of its life history then it has forfeited a chance to learn and grow. Recidivism or repeating past behaviors might be a survival mechanism or it may be self-defeating, or it may be neither – just laziness in which the current environment can tolerate.

What if the individual recedes prior to being born? What happens if it is born with a more ancestral form? This atavism is a resurfacing of form and function lost and unknown to the present. It is a resurfacing of an old text buried on a palimpsest long ago erased, written over and suddenly discovered among the latest layer of recent text. Does this atavistic text make sense within the context of the new writings? Does it still have meaning? Is the atavistic form and function adaptive in the current environment?

Fowler uses the sexuality of the bonobo to inform the pornography of the human. The same behavior accepted within the norms of our recent cousin the bonobo, is judged to be pornographic in humans. It is at once recidivistic behavior in the individual and atavistic in the human populations. Using recidivism and atavism as different lenses to focus on sexuality, he challenges the interpretation of what is pornographic. If the same behavior can be normal in one situation but pornographic in another, doesn't that say more about the environment?

Here is a palimpsest working as the link connecting the evolution of literature to the literature of evolution. It is the metaphor to carry the subtle shift in understanding between recidivism and atavism. The palimpsest sets any text or any trait with a history unfolding over time, constantly being effaced and rewritten, hidden and re-emerging.

Works Cited

Meredith L Chivers and others, 'Gender and sexual orientation differences in sexual response to sexual activities versus gender of actors in sexual films', *Journal of Personality and Social Psychology:* vol. 93,6 (2007): 1108-21. doi:10.1037/0022-3514.93.6.1108

Dalke, Anne and Paul Grobstein, 'The Story of Evolution and the Evolution of Stories', Serendip, <https://serendipstudio.org/exchange/courses/evolit/s09> [accessed 15th September 2023]

Darwin, Charles, *The Variation of Animals and Plants Under Domestication*, second edition, (London: John Murray, 1868)

Fowler, SJ, *The Great Apes*, (Rhydwen, Wales: Broken Sleep Books, 2022).

Gould, Stephen Jay, *Hen's Teeth and Horse's Toes: Further Reflections in Natural History*, Reissue Edition, (New York City, New York: W.W.Norton & Company, 1994)

'Recidivism', *Oxford English Dictionary*, Oxford University Press < https://www.oed.com/dictionary/recidivism_n?tab=meaning_and_use#26568127> [accessed 1st June 2023]

Winterson, Jeanette, *Written on the Body*, (New York City: Vintage, 1994) p. 20.

www.ingramcontent.com/pod-product-compliance
Lightning Source LLC
Chambersburg PA
CBHW011759040426
42446CB00019B/3462